Cheyne Publications,
94 Cheyne Walk,
London SW10 ODQ

ISBN 0 9527409 0 7

Drawings by Alice Scrutton, Fairfax Gallery, The Pantiles, Tunbridge Wells, Kent.

Printed by APR Printing and Design Ltd. Uckfield. East Sussex TN22 5AH

i

Simon Scrutton
was for over 20 years
Chef/Proprietor of
the national award-winning
Byrons Restaurant
in Sussex.

Preface

It is with considerable relief and not a little excitement that I finally see this volume to bed. To squeeze the writing of a book into the normal working life of a chef, needs a lot of determination. Fate, however, came to my rescue; in the form of a broken arm! So what has been promised to my friends, for so long, has had many weeks to blossom.

It is curious how, when eating in a restaurant, one expects even quite complicated dishes to appear quickly - as if by magic. Accomplished cooks too, can forget the intensity of labour and time involved and are as impatient as the next man when their apple tart takes 20 minutes. But these same people would be horrified if they thought their meal had been prepared in advance for the sake of speedy service.

Restaurants have to develop tricks to minimise these problems, while still producing fresh and delicious food. I have tried to pass on a few of these secrets in this book.

All the recipes can be either prepared in advance up to a certain point (for each recipe, I have clearly shown where this point is), or are quick to cook 'a la minute'; leaving the maximum time to relax with your guests.

Many recipes necessitate the use of a food processor or powerful liquidizer. A Mouli-Legume (only a few pounds from cookery shops) is useful; and a deep fryer is needed for one or two dishes.

An oven thermometer is a good investment, as ovens can vary in heat amazingly. Sensitive dishes, like Spinach Mousse (q.v.), can become disasters if cooked at the wrong temperature.

Recipes are given in both Imperial and Metric measurements. Either use one set or the other, but don't mix them up.

Marinated Black Olives

This delicious preparation needs olives of a certain type (not bitter Greek wrinklies) to be a success. The best widely available are Sainsbury's own brand of tinned black olives. These are either the same or similar to Moroccan olives sold under the brand name Crespo.

INGREDIENTS:

1 400g tin of Black Olives (pitted or otherwise) - or your favourite loose olives; drained

1 medium clove of Garlic, peeled and chopped

1 pinch of Dried Thyme

3 tablespoons(3 × 15ml) Sunflower/Groundnut/Good Olive Oil

METHOD:

1. Mix the drained olives with the other ingredients.

Ideal with drinks or to serve before a meal.

Will keep for up to 1 month in a fridge in a covered plastic container or glass jar.

Cheese Straws

Very good with drinks and easy to make.

INGREDIENTS FOR ABOUT 50 STRAWS:

3 oz(90g) Plain Flour, sieved

3 oz(90g) Butter, at room temperature

1 × No.2 or 2 × No. 4 Egg Yolks

2 oz(60g) Strong Cheddar Cheese, grated

1 oz(30g) Fresh Parmesan Cheese, grated

$^1/_4$ teaspoon(1ml) Chilli Powder

$^1/_4$ teaspoon(1ml) Fine Salt.

METHOD:

1. Put the butter into a large bowl and cream until light.

2. Add the flour, egg yolk, salt and chilli powder to the butter and mix together thoroughly.

3. Mix in the grated cheese.

4. Gather the dough into a ball, put into a plastic bag or wrap in clingfilm, then rest in the fridge for about 30 minutes.

5. Heat the oven to Gas 5, 375F, 190C.

6. Roll out the dough, on a lightly floured surface, until about $^1/_4$ in(50mm) thick.

7. Cut the dough into long fingers - any leftovers can be re-rolled, so you should be able to use it all.

8. Transfer carefully to a baking tray, giving each a little twist if you like.

9. Bake in the oven for about 10 - 15 minutes, or until golden.

Cool a little, then taste to make sure they're alright. When you've finished them, start again!

Better warm, but still good cold. Keep in an air-tight tin.

Chilled Celery Soup, with Fennel and Dill.

For vegetarians, the chicken stock can be replaced with two vegetable stock cubes dissolved in 2.5 pints(1.4l) water - I think that Knorr are easily the best.

EQUIPMENT -

A food processor, liquidiser or Mouli-Legume.

INGREDIENTS -

2 oz(80g) Butter

1 good head of Celery (including leaves) chopped

4 oz(160g) of raw Potato, peeled and chopped

1 medium clove of Garlic, chopped

4 oz(160g) Onion, chopped

2.5 pints(1.4l) of homemade Chicken Stock (q.v) - or 2 Knorr Chicken Stock Cubes dissolved, over a low heat, in 2.5 pints of water

$^1/_2$ pint(300ml) of Single Cream

8 Fennel Seeds (available dried from supermarkets)

1 sprig of fresh Dillweed (available in the summer from good supermarkets)

Salt and Pepper, to taste.

METHOD -

1. Gently melt the butter in a saucepan, big enough to hold all the ingredients.

2. Add the chopped celery, potato, onion and garlic. *Sweat* for about 10 minutes, stirring occasionally.

3. Add the fennel and dillseeds, then the stock and bring slowly to the boil. Simmer for 40 minutes, stirring occasionally.

4. Remove from the heat and remove the dillweed.

5. Liquidise the mixture, or pass through a Mouli-Legume.

6. Add the cream; and salt and pepper to taste - remembering that cold food tends to lose flavour. Mix well.

7. Chill; then serve with a bowl of *croutons*.

* *This soup can be prepared the day before you need it, indeed the flavour will improve.*

Whereas the Chilled Celery Soup takes a little time to prepare, the following recipe is embarrassingly quick and easy - but amazingly delicious. Do not give your secret away!

Under no circumstances be tempted to use dried basil, as the result will be very disappointing.

Chilled Tomato and Basil Soup

EQUIPMENT
A food processor or liquidizer.

INGREDIENTS -
2 × 14 oz(400g) tins of Tomatoes (Italian seem to always have the best flavour)

4-6 leaves of fresh Basil (depending on size)

1 big, or 2 small, cloves of Garlic, peeled and chopped

$^1/_2$pint (300ml) of Plain Yoghurt

1 teaspoon of Caster Sugar

The juice of 1/2 Lemon

Salt and freshly ground Black Pepper, to taste

$^1/_4$ of a Cucumber, very thinly sliced (optional)

A bowl of small *croutons* (optional).

METHOD -
1. Process all the ingredients together in a Food Processor
2. Refrigerate until well chilled.
3. Test the seasoning
4. Serve, decorated with the thin cucumber slices and hand round the croutons.

What could be easier?

Pistou Soup

This soup comes from the borders of Italy and south-east France; an area that has changed allegiance many times. It is particularly delicious with a little Pesto Sauce (q.v) stirred into each bowl just before serving. This soup is ideal for vegetarians, and with Pesto added, should satisfy any garlic lover too!

INGREDIENTS FOR 6 GENEROUS HELPINGS -
2oz(60g) dried white Haricot Beans, soaked in cold water for 6 hours, then boiled for 10 minutes and drained

$^3/_4$lb(360g) of baby Kenya green beans, headed and tailed, then cut into 1 inch lengths

2 big Potatoes, peeled and diced

1 × 14oz(**400g**) tin of chopped tomatoes

3 small, firm, very green Courgettes, *diced*

2 tablespoons of dried Vermicelli Pasta

4.25 pints(2l) cold water

1 large Onion, peeled and chopped

1 big, or 2 medium, cloves of garlic, peeled and chopped

3 tablespoons of good Olive Oil

Salt and freshly ground Black Pepper

1 batch of Pesto Sauce (q.v).

METHOD -

1. In a big pan, large enough to hold all the ingredients, heat the olive oil gently, then *sweat* the chopped onion and garlic until the onion is soft (do not burn the garlic, or it will become bitter)
2. Add the *blanched* haricot beans, the chopped green beans, potatoes and tomatoes; mix thoroughly. Do not add the courgettes at this stage
3. Cover with the water, bring to the boil, and *simmer* for 30 minutes
4. Now add the courgettes and vermicelli and cook for a further 5 minutes
5. Add the salt and pepper (only a little, as your guests can always add more). Add a little Pesto Sauce to each bowl and stir well in. Extra Pesto should be placed in a bowl on the table, so that your guests can help themselves.

This soup can be prepared ahead to this stage and reheated successfully, but do not overcook, or you will lose the beautiful colour. If reheating, do not add any pesto until just before serving.

Curried Parsnip Soup

A delicious soup made popular by Jane Grigson; also beautifully easy to make. For a special occasion accompany with parsnip crisps: see Crisps from Root Vegetables (q.v.).

INGREDIENTS FOR 6:

6 oz(170ml) Butter
2 lb(900g) Parsnips, peeled and chopped
1 medium Onion, peeled and chopped
1 Leek, carefully washed and chopped
2 big or 4 medium cloves of Garlic, peeled and chopped
1 tablespoon(15ml) Flour
3 teaspoons(3 × 5ml) Curry Powder
4 pints(2.2l) Beef or Vegetable Stock
10 fl.oz(280ml) Single Cream
Salt and freshly ground Pepper
Chopped fresh Chives (optional).
Equipment: Food Processor or Liquidizer

METHOD:

1. *Sweat* the vegetables in the butter for 15 minutes, turning occasionally.
2. Add the flour and curry powder - mix well in.
3. Gradually add the stock, stirring all the time.
4. Bring the soup to the boil and *simmer* until the parsnip is tender - about 20 minutes.
5. Remove from the heat and allow to cool slightly.
6. Liquidize.
7. Add the cream, then check the seasoning, adding salt and pepper as necessary.
   Can be prepared ahead up to this point.
Serve sprinkled with chives.

Mediterranean Fish Soup

Please read this introduction carefully, because although it looks lengthy, and the making of this soup may look daunting, the dish is an easy one to prepare (as is everything in this book); and while it is cooking your kitchen will be full of the most beautiful smells.

Personally speaking, this is my favourite soup, and would certainly include it if I had to chose a desert island meal.

Restaurant chefs are in the lucky position of handling many types of fish over a short period of time; so can save up heads and bones, as well as lobster and crab shells in the deep freeze.

These can be released from their suspended state at an opportune moment, to make a delicious soup.

Do not be disheartened, ask your fishmonger if he will save an assortment of bones (smartly known as frames in the trade) in his deep-freeze for you. Most fishmongers will be pleased for the interest shown, particularly if you are a regular customer, and be only too willing to oblige. Also of value are fish that are either damaged, or so small as to be of little value to anyone else. As well as your scraps and frames what you need is some soft fleshed fish, a dab or plaice is ideal, plus some pieces of a firmer type - perhaps cod, haddock or conger eel. Avoid oily fish, such as herring, salmon or mackerel. If you can find a whole crab, even better - have it split and the inedible stomach removed. A few shell-on prawns add a marvellous flavour, and a baby red mullet or gurnard would be a real coup.

A more than satisfactory soup can be made with a few bones plus one or two types of the fish listed, as long as you add my three most important ingredients - these are Orange Peel, Leek and Fennel!

Suprised?

I'm sure you are, but these three ingredients will give your soup great depth of flavour.

EQUIPMENT:

A food processor or Braun liquidizing rod.

INGREDIENTS: (FOR 8 PEOPLE)

3fl oz(90ml) good Olive Oil

2 big or 4 medium cloves of Garlic, peeled and chopped

4 oz(120g) each of Fennel (bulb not seed), Leek, Celery and Carrot, all chopped

1/2 pint(300ml) of Dry White Wine

1 sherry glass of Pernod or Ricard, or 2 pieces of Star Anise (available on the spice racks of good supermarkets, or from a delicatessen)

1 × 14oz(400g) tin of chopped Italian tomatoes

5oz(150g) of Tomato Puree

1 good pinch of Saffron strands, or a little packet of powder (saffron can seem frightlingly expensive but a little goes a very long way)

2 big pieces (about 1/2 an orange worth) of Orange Rind, make sure that you remove as much white pith as possible, as it leaves a bitter taste

1 level teaspoon of mixed Herbes de Provence: the best of these contain lavender and green anise

2 Bay leaves

Approximately 2lbs(1 kilo) of mixed fish (as explained above), washed to remove any blood

An old lobster shell, kept in the deep-freeze from a previous meal (optional)

4oz(120g) of shell-on North Atlantic Prawns

1 whole cooked Crab (if you can find one), split and cleaned (the stomach removed) by your fishmonger. Break this up further yourself, by removing the legs then putting in a plastic bag and hitting hard with a hanner or rolling pin (this will allow all the flavour to be released)

6 pints(3.5l) of cold water

A little (about ⅛th of a teaspoon of Cayenne Pepper.

If possible (but a luxury) about the same quantity of mixed heads and frames (again thoroughly washed)

Salt and freshly ground Black Pepper, to taste.

To serve: You will need some Rouille (q.v), grated Fresh Parmesan (on no account be tempted to use dried) and some *Croutes*.

METHOD:

1. Gently heat the olive oil in a big pan, big and deep enough to hold all the ingredients; then add the chopped mixed vegetables and garlic - *sweat* them until they start to soften, about 5 minutes.

2. *Deglaze* the pan with the wine and the Pernod/Ricard (if using); allow the mixture to bubble for a few minutes.

3. Add the remaining ingredients, with the exception of the salt, pepper and cayenne.

4. Bring the mixture to the boil, then reduce the heat and *simmer* for about an hour, uncovered.

Fish Soup - continued:

5. Remove from the heat and carefully take out any big fish bones, plus crab and lobster shells (if you've managed to procure any) - basically anything sturdy enough to damage a food processor - so small fish bones, and certainly prawns, should stay in.

6. Liquidize the soup, either in batches in a food processor, or by using a Braun hand-held liquidizing rod. Either way process until you have a fairly smooth liquid. The small pieces of fish and vegetables will act as a thickening agent.

7. When your soup is fairly smooth, pass it through a course sieve or colander; working as many of the solid ingredients through as you can, using the bottom of a strong ladle, or the back of a wooden spoon. Basically the more goodies you force through the straining system, the thicker (and more delicious) your soup will be. You should be aiming for a consistency resembling tinned tomato soup.

8. Add salt, pepper and the cayenne pepper to taste - remembering that the strength of the cayenne will increase, particularly if you are making your soup a day ahead.

Serve with Rouille (q.v) some grated fresh Parmesan and some croutes, cut on the diagonal from a french stick, and either oven-dried or toasted.

As I'm sure you know, the idea is that you spread the rouille onto a croute, float it on top of your bowl of soup, then sprinkle some cheese over the top.

This combination is suprisingly delicious and can be repeated as many times as you like - so allow 3 or croutes per person.

As well as being delicious, this soup is filling and if served with plenty of french bread, makes a meal on it's own. Although the recipe seems long, if you save up your fish over a period of time, the cooking process is very easy and only needs concentrated attention at the sieving stage.

Warm Spinach Mousse

A firm favourite of mine for more years than I care to remember. Whatever restaurant I have cooked in I have been loath to take this off the menu, for fear of having to face extremely upset customers.

One of the problems in trying to work out a restaurant menu is the balancing act of, on the one hand introducing new dishes, and on the other satisfying customers who might dine two or three times a year (and who would consider themselves regulars) and always want to eat the same thing.

There is a strong case to be made for restaurants sticking to what they're best at. Change for it's own sake is not commendable.

You can make this recipe your own; and your guests too, will want it every time they eat with you.

I have experimented with every type of Spinach, from frozen leaf to fresh; easily the best results are obtained from either frozen puree, or frozen nuggets, which many supermarkets now sell.

EQUIPMENT:

Food processor; 4 - 6 ramekins (depending on size); tin foil for covering.

INGREDIENTS FOR 4 - 6:

12oz(340g) frozen Spinach puree - thawed, then left to drain in a sieve

12 fl.oz(340ml) Single Cream

1 × No.3 Egg.

Salt, Pepper and plenty of freshly grated Nutmeg (perhaps 6-8 good strokes of the grater)

A little softened butter, for buttering the ramekins.

METHOD:

1. Squeeze as much moisture as possible out of the spinach.
2. Butter 4 ramekins, or similar ovenproof containers.
3. Put the spinach in a food processor, then add the remaining ingredients.
4. Process until well mixed.
5. Distribute the mixture between the ramekins and cover each with a square of tin foil, which should be tucked neatly around the rim of the ramekins to form a good seal. This will prevent the mousses drying out on top.
6. Pierce a small hole in each foil lid, to allow any steam to escape during cooking.

* At this point the mousses can be refrigerated, overnight if need be.

7. Heat the oven to Gas 4, 350F, 180C. Place the ramekins on a baking tray, and cook in the preheated oven for 40 minutes. For small mousses such as these, there is no need to surround them with water. In fact don't be tempted to do so, for it will change the cooking time.
8. Remove from the oven. The mousses should have risen slightly and be firm to the touch. If not, cook for 5 minutes more.
9. Carefully remove the foil hats and allow the mousses to cool for 5 minutes. Don't be alarmed if they sink back a little!
10. Run a sharp knife around the edge of each mousse and turn out onto individual warm serving plates.

Serve covered with a little Fresh Parmesan or Anchovy Sauce (q.v).

Artichokes Nissarda

I first tried this delicious starter at Langan's Brasserie in London, where it had been introduced by the chef Richard Shepherd; based on a recipe he had found in Nice.

It is composed of 3 parts -

1. One or more Artichoke Bottoms, as a base.

2. A Duxelle of mushrooms, as stuffing.

3. Either Hollandaise or Bearnaise Sauces (q.v.) to complete.

The correct way of making this dish is to prepare fresh globe artichokes, which although producing a slightly better flavour, is too drawn out for most of you at home.

What I suggest is that you buy a tin of artichoke bottoms (not hearts) at your local supermarket or delicatessen.

These are not expensive, perhaps a quarter of the price of buying fresh artichokes and will cut out fiddly preparation.

I can see gourmets holding their heads in their hands at this suggestion, but once the dish has been finished it would take an experienced professional to tell fresh from tinned.

INGREDIENTS:

1 or 2 tins of Artichoke Bottoms, depending on greed

6 oz(170g) Flat Mushrooms - button and cup varieties lack flavour and produce a grey coloured duxelle

2 oz(56g) peeled and roughly chopped Onion

1 slice of de-rinded and finely chopped Streaky Bacon (optional)

1 oz(28g) Butter or 1 tablespoon Olive Oil

Salt and freshly ground Black Pepper

One batch of Hollandaise or Bearnaise Sauce (q.v.)

A little finely chopped Parsley, to decorate.

METHOD:

1. Drain the artichoke bottoms and rinse thoroughly in cold water. Decide if you are giving one, two or three each. Three would make an excellent light lunch with some good French bread.

2. Place the artichoke bottoms on to an ovenproof dish and pre-heat the oven to Gas 3,325F, 160C. If you have a microwave oven, you can use this instead.

3. Put the onions and mushrooms in a food processor and chop until finely diced, but not a puree. This is best done by continually turning the machine on and off, or using a Pulse switch if you have one.

4. Place the butter or oil in a saucepan and heat gently. Lightly fry the bacon (if using), then add your mushroom mixture. Mushrooms always produce quite a lot of liquid, so stir occasionally and cook until most of this has evaporated and the mixture has become firmer. Add a little salt and pepper.

5. Stuff the artichoke bottoms with the mushroom mixture.

* Can be prepared ahead up to this stage. The sauce can also be made as directed.

6. If serving now place in the pre-heated oven for a few minutes to heat the artichokes, while you are making the sauce.

Share the artichokes out between your guests plates, covering each with a little sauce and a sprinkling of chopped parsley.

Don't tell anyone that you've used tinned chokes, they will never know!

Mushroom and Walnut Pate.

Mushrooms and Walnuts have a tremendous affinity for one another and this clever pate is marvellous if one has one or two vegetarians in the party as the definite flavours leave the carnivores feeling satisfied too!

EQUIPMENT:

Food processor.

INGREDIENTS:

4 oz(110g) Onion, peeled

1 medium clove of Garlic, peeled

2 tablespoons Sunflower Oil

8 oz(225g) Flat Mushrooms (buttons and cups don't have enough flavour)

A few fresh marjoram leaves or a few torn leaves of fresh Basil (do not use dried)

1.5 oz(40g) Walnut halves or pieces

Salt and freshly ground Black Pepper

METHOD:

1. Finely chop the onion and garlic in the food processor then *sweat* in the oil until soft (about 5 minutes), do not allow to brown.

2. Chop the mushrooms in the processor, a few at a time.

3. Add the mushrooms and your chosen herb to the onions. They will produce some liquid - cook over a medium heat until this has evaporated, stirring occasionally; remove from the heat.

4. Process the walnuts until finely chopped and then add them to the mushroom mixture.

5. Add Salt and pepper to taste. Refrigerate.

Serve the pate with toast and unsalted butter.

Warm Tart of Saffron and Brie

Another filling for the excellent Garlic and Sherry Pastry (q.v.) tarts. Again quite filling enough for a light lunch.

INGREDIENTS FOR FOUR:

4 oz(120g) Brie, roughly chopped

4 oz(120g) Curd Cheese

2 tablespoons(2 × 15ml) Clear Honey

2 × No.3 Eggs

A big pinch of Saffron Strands, soaked in a tablespoon(15ml) of very hot water for 15 minutes.

6 fl.oz(170ml) Double Cream

Salt and freshly ground Pepper.

$^1/_2$ Batch of Garlic and Sherry Pastry (q.v.)

METHOD:

1. Follow all the steps for preparing Rainbow Trout and Spring Onion Tart (q.v.).

The addition of potted shrimps however, would not be a good idea!

Chinese Prawn and Sesame Toasts

These will probably be one of the most popular starters/drinks nibbles that you have ever made. They will certainly be better than the ones produced by your local Chinese restaurant, where they will sometimes be greasy and invariably re-heated.

They can, on the other hand, be prepared well ahead of time, as long as the final frying is done at the last minute.

You will achieve the best results with bread that is less than fresh, as it will absorb less oil. You can always dry the slices out slightly in the oven.

EQUIPMENT:

A food processor; a Deep-fryer with clean oil, or 8 tablespoons of frying oil & a deep frying pan.

INGREDIENTS FOR THE PASTE TOPPING:

4 Spring Onions

A ³/₄in piece of Root Ginger, peeled and roughly chopped

1 × No 3 Egg

1 lb(480g) peeled North Atlantic Prawns

1 rounded tablespoon of cornflour

2 fl oz(60g) Crème Fraîche or Plain Yoghurt

1 tablespoon of light soy sauce

For the assembly: about 10 slices of thin-sliced white bread, with the crusts removed &
4 tablespoons of white Sesame Seeds.

METHOD:

1. Finely chop the onions with the root ginger in a food processor.

2. Add all the other Paste Topping ingredients and blend until very smooth.

3. Spread the paste generously between the bread slices, then cover thoroughly with the sesame seeds. This is best done by spreading the seeds
onto a baking tray, then inverting your bread slices
onto the seeds.

4, Cut each slice of bread into 4 triangles, or into fingers if you prefer.

* At this stage your toasts can be refrigerated until needed; overnight if need be.

5. To finish: either deep-fry them at 325F,160C, or heat some oil in a big frying pan, until a haze rises, then fry them paste side down for 2-3 minutes, then turn them over and fry for a further 2 minutes, or until golden brown. Keep repeating the process until they are all done.

Drain on kitchen paper and serve warm.

Warm Tart of Rainbow Trout and Spring Onions

Delicious starter and quite filling enough for the basis of a light lunch. These tarts need no attention during their 30 minute baking time - and can be prepared, up to this point, a day ahead.

EQUIPMENT:
Individual tart tins, loose-bottomed if possible.

INGREDIENTS FOR FOUR.
1 × 8 oz(230g) Trout Fillet, skinned and cut into 2 in(45mm) pieces

1 Spring Onion, washed and chopped into small pieces

2 oz(60g) Cottage Cheese, drained of any excess liquid

1 × No.3 Egg, lightly beaten

2 fl.oz(50ml) Single Cream or Milk

A little Salt and freshly ground Pepper

$^1/_2$ batch of Garlic Pastry (q.v.)

A little soft Butter to smear around tart tins.

METHOD:
1. Line the lightly buttered tart tins with the pastry.

2. Prick all over the bases with a fork and chill for a minimum of 30 minutes (overnight if need be).

3. Prepare the stuffing by mixing together all the filling ingredients. Chill until needed.

4. Pre-heat the oven to Gas 6, 400F, 200C.

5. Bake the pastry cases *blind* for 15 minutes; remove from the oven and loosen the pastry in the tins.

* Can be prepared in advance up to this point.

6. Light or adjust the oven to Gas 3, 324F, 160C.

7. Share the trout filling between the tarts, being careful not to spill any - if it overflows the tarts can become stuck in their tins.

8. Bake for 30 minutes.

To serve; allow to cool slightly, then remove tarts from their tins. A little salad decoration sets them off well.

Variation:
A baby tub of Potted Shrimps added to the trout mixture makes a scrumptious addition.

Mussels

As well as being cheap, mussels are cheap and very easy to prepare. They are completely safe as long as you follow two simple rules.

1. Never gather your own mussels from the sea. Although nine times out of ten they might be fine, the risk is not worth taking. Poisoning from just a few bad or contaminated mussels can be very severe. Mussels bought from a fishmonger are very cheap, generally free of barnicles and will have spent time in a purifying tank before going on sale.

2. Always rinse your mussels in plenty of running water, just before cooking. Tap any open shells on the edge of the sink, any that refuse to close should be thrown away. The thinking behind this is that mussels deteriorate fairly quickly after death and you have no way of knowing how long an open mussel has been dead - so for safety reasons only closed (alive) mussels are cooked.

A pint of mussels will give a generous starter-sized helping for each person. The smaller ones, commonly found in northern France (and frequently imported) have a sweeter flavour, but the larger ones are much less work!

Moules Mariniere

This classic dish is so often ruined by cheaper restaurants, who - for the sake of a little time - cook it ahead and serve it re-heated. The mussels not only lose their fresh colour, but they also become overcooked.

INGREDIENTS:

4 pints(2.25kilos) fresh Mussels

2 oz(60g) Unsalted Butter

Large pinch of dried thyme, or 1 sprig of fresh

2 teaspoons(2 × 5ml) freshly chopped Parsley, plus a little for decoration

2 oz(60g) finely chopped onions or shallots

2-3 cloves of Garlic, peeled and chopped

The juice of 1 lemon, sieved

$1/4$ pint(140ml) Dry White Wine

$1/4$ pint(140ml) Cold Water

Freshly ground Black Pepper.

METHOD:

1. Under cold running water, scrape the mussel shells free of sand and barnicles and pull off the beard - which looks like a little piece of attached seaweed. Discard any which stay open when tapped hard; or any that are cracked or feel unnaturally heavy - as these could be full of mud or sand.

This is a labourious task in a restaurant, but quite quick for only four people.

2. Put all the ingredients, except the mussels and your parsley for decoration, in a very large saucepan which has a close-fitting lid.

* Can be prepared a few hours in advance up to this stage and kept in a cool place.

3. Bring the mixture to the boil, then simmer for 2 minutes.

4. Add the mussels and cover with the lid. Cook them for 2 minutes, on a high heat, shaking the saucepan vigorously several times.

5. Have a look - they should now be open. If not, cook them (with the lid on) for a further minute.

6. Remove the mussels from the pan and share them between 4 previously warmed bowls, pouring the juices over them. Be careful with the last bit, in case it's a bit gritty.

Sprinkle with the remaining Parsley and serve with good French Bread.

Variations of Moules Mariniere -

Moules A La Creme

INGREDIENTS:

As for Moules Mariniere plus:

5 fl.oz(140ml) Double Cream or Creme Fraiche

METHOD:

1. Wash, clean and cook mussels as for Moules Mariniere and share them without their juices between 4 bowls: discarding any that do not open.

2. Add the cream or creme fraiche to the pan and cook for a further minute.

3. For a smarter dish the empty mussel shell can be removed and the shells lain flat to hold the sauce.

Check the seasonings and pour over the shellfish.

A little Pernod/ Ricard or Curry Powder can be added with the cream to make a delicious change.

Moules Provencal

INGREDIENTS:

48 Mussels

1 batch of Garlic Butter (q.v.)

1 oz(30g) Fresh Breadcrumbs

METHOD:

1. Clean and wash the mussels, as for Moules Mariniere.

2. Place them in a stainless steel saucepan with a close fitting lid.

3. Add 2 tablespoons of water and put over a high heat. Shake occasionally, after 4-5 minutes they should be open; remove from the heat and allow to cool in the covered saucepan for a further 2 minutes. Discard any mussels that have not opened.

4. Lift the mussels out of their liquid, break them in half - throwing the empty shell away.

5. Put a good teaspoonful of garlic butter on each mussel, transfer them to a baking tray or individual ovenproof plates.

6. Sprinkle the breadcrumbs over the top.

* Can be prepared ahead of time up to this point and refrigerated.

7. Heat in a pre-heated oven Gas 6, 400F, 200C for 5-6 minutes.

Serve with plenty of French bread to mop up the juices.

Mejillones Al Vapor

A simple method of cooking mussels from the Alicante region of Spain.

INGREDIENTS:
2 tablespoons(2 × 15ml) Olive Oil
48 fresh Mussels
Juice of 2 Lemons, sieved
Freshly ground Fresh Pepper

METHOD:
1. Clean and wash the mussels as in Stage 1 of Moules Mariniere.
2. Heat the oil gently in a big pan - wide enough for all the mussels to touch the bottom.
3. Add the mussels, lemon juice and pepper - salt will come out of the shellfish, so no more is needed.
4. Cover and cook over a high heat, shaking the pan occasionally, for about 3 minutes - or until all the mussels have opened: discard any mussels that do not open.

Serve hot in individual bowls with any juice from the pan poured over them. Alternatively serve cold with Garlic Vinaigrette or Aioli (q.v.).

The following two recipes are easy to prepare and will give a far-eastern flavour to your mussels.

Thai Mussels

INGREDIENTS.
4 pints(2.25kilos) fresh Mussels
6 cloves fresh Garlic, peeled and chopped
2 tablespoons(2 × 15ml) Groundnut Oil
1 large Red Chilli, de-seeded and chopped (wash your handed thoroughly after doing this)
2 tablespoons(2 × 15ml) Nam Pla Sauce - easily available from oriental specialist food shop
A small bunch of chopped fresh mint or basil leaves.

METHOD:
1. Clean the mussels, as for Moules Mariniere (q.v.)
2. Heat the oil over a medium heat in a big deep pan, which has a close-fitting lid.
3. Add the chopped garlic an chilli, followed 2 minutes later by the nam pla sauce. Mix well.
4. Add the mussels, cover with the lid and increase the heat to high.
5. Cook for 2-3 minutes shaking occasionally; the mussels should now be open. Throw away any that resolutely stay closed.
6. Remove the shellfish from their juices and discard the empty half of each shell.
7. Share the mussel-filled halves between 4 serving bowls.
8. Add the mint or basil to the remaining sauce and pour over the mussels.

Chinese Mussels

INGREDIENTS:

4 pints(2.25kilos) fresh Mussels

2 tablespoons(2 × 15ml) Sunflower or Groundnut Oil

2 tablespoons(2 × 15ml) Tomato Puree

4 tablespoons(4 × 15ml) Dry White Wine

2 teaspoons(2 × 5ml) Caster Sugar

4 teaspoons(4 × 5ml) Dark Soy Sauce

4 Chillies, de-seeded and thinly sliced (wash your hands after touching these)

1 tablespoon(1 × 15ml) chopped fresh ginger

4 cloves of Garlic, peeled and chopped

1 tablespoon(1 × 15ml) Cornflour

6 tablespoons(6 × 15ml) cold Water

6 Spring Onions, cleaned and sliced on the diagonal.

METHOD:

1. Clean and wash the mussels as in Stage 1 of Moules Mariniere (q.v.)

2. Heat the oil in a big pan, with a close fitting lid.

3. Add the mussels, cover and cook over a high heat for 2-3 minutes, shaking vigorously occasionally. The shellfish should be open - close any that resolutely stay closed.

4. Share the mussels between 4 serving bowls, removing the empty half-shells if prefered.

5. Lower the heat, then add the chillis, ginger and garlic; cook gently for 2 minutes in the remaining oil and mussel juices. Add the tomato puree, wine, sugar and soy sauce.

6. Dissolve the cornflour in the cold water, stirring to remove any lumps. Add this to the sauce.

7. Cook until the mixture thickens - about 2-3 minutes.

8. Add the sliced spring onions, mix well, then pour over the mussels.

Sardines with a Sicilian Stuffing

This easy to make stuffing will give you the most delicious sardines you have ever tasted. The quantity given is sufficient for 26-28 Sardines, but as it's very cheap to make, its hardly worth messing around with a smaller quantity.

First prepare your stuffing: this can be done a day ahead (in fact the flavour will improve), then refrigerated. Bring it back to room temperature for half an hour, or so, before using, so that it is manageable.

INGREDIENTS:

4 oz(120g) fresh white breadcumbs - these are easily made in a food processor (but remove the crusts, as they make reluctant crumbs!)

2 tablespoons(2 × 15ml) good Olive Oil

3 medium cloves of Garlic, peeled a and chopped

2 tablespoons(2 × 15ml) chopped Parsley

2 tablespoons(2 × 15ml) peeled and chopped shallots/mild onions

Juice of half a lemon

Food Processor or big pestle and mortar. A heatproof bowl that neatly fits over a saucepan to form a *bain-marie*.

2 oz(60g), chopped Capers

2 oz(60g), chopped Black Olives: Sainsbury's own-brand tins of olives are excellent

2 oz(50g) chopped Sultanas

2 oz(50g) chopped Pine nut Kernels

4 Anchovy Fillets, chopped

A little salt and plenty of freshly ground Black Pepper

METHOD:

1. Mix all the ingredients together.

To fillet Sardines:

This is much easier and less fiddly than you would imagine.

I. Split the sardine, either head on or decapitated, from head to tail along their stomachs.

2. Place, cut side down, on a plate and gently but firmly push down to butterfly the fish - concentrating any pressure along the backbone.

3. Turn the fish over: the backbone will be loose and can be pulled out with the mildest pressure - simply snapping it off just before the head and tail.

Your fish is now ready to stuff.

In Sicily, this is usually done (to headless fish) by spreading the stuffing thinly over the fish and then rolling them up lengthways towards the tail. I usually insert the stuffing in the normal way (so they look like fish).

* Can be prepared a day ahead up to this point and keep cling-wrapped in the fridge.

The Sicilians then drizzle them with olive oil and bake in a hot oven for about 8 minutes.

I simply grill or barbecue them for a few minutes on each side.

Either way, serve with plenty of lemon wedges and you will have compliments galore!

Brandade of Smoked Mackerel in Puff Pastry

In this dish, which is guaranteed to impress your friends, the cod in traditional Brandade (q.v.) has been replaced by smoked mackerel to make an unusual filling for little pastry puffs. The quantity given will serve about six people. They freeze well and are a good standby, as they are just as successful cooked straight from the freezer.

Delicious with Cucumber Raita - see below.

EQUIPMENT:

Food Processor or big pestle and mortar. A heatproof bowl that neatly fits over a saucepan to form a *bain-marie*.

INGREDIENTS: (FOR SIX)

2 cloves of Garlic, peeled
Very little Salt (as smoked mackerel is already salty)
8 oz(230g) Smoked Mackerel Fillets, skinned
2 fl.oz(60ml) Milk
2 fl.oz(60ml) good Olive Oil
Freshly ground Black Pepper
Juice of ¹/₂ Lemon, sieved
About 12 oz(400g) bought Puff Pastry; gently thawed if frozen
About 2 oz(50g) Flour (for rolling out the pastry and lining the baking trays
1 Egg, lightly beaten.

METHOD:

1. Chop the garlic finely in a food processor with a little salt to melt it.

2. Add the mackerel fillets and process until the mixture is smooth.

3. Prepare a *bain-marie* and in it warm the mackerel paste.

4. Have the milk and oil ready in two cups or jugs and add these alternately, a little at a time; mix well with a wooden spoon to incorporate each addition.

5. Don't let the mixture get too hot, it should just stay warm.

6. Season to taste with pepper, then add the lemon juice. On no account add extra salt.

7. Chill in the fridge for a minimum of an hour - the mixture will happily keep for a few days if covered. Some oil might separate, but will just need beating back in.

* A prolonged rest may be taken at this point.

8. Roll out the puff pastry fairly thinly, using a little of the flour to stop it sticking.

9. Stamp out rounds of about 3 ins(7.5cm) across, with a pastry cutter or glass. Any leftover pastry can be re-rolled to make more puffs.

10. Put a generous teaspoonful (8ml) of mackerel mixture on each round of pastry, then brush the edges of the dough with a little water; fold the pastry over to make a little purse and carefully seal with your fingers. The edges can be crimped with the prongs of a fork to produce a professional result.

* Can be prepared ahead up to this point: if doing this read the following two paragraphs.

11. Keep the baby pasties on a lightly floured tray in the fridge for up to two days - or freeze on a tray: when frozen they can be stored in a plastic bag in the deep freeze and cooked as required.

To flour a tray - rub it all over with a cold block of butter, then distribute the flour over it (by gently tapping) - any excess flour can be removed (for use on the next tray). The benefit of this system is that there is no surplus flour left to stick to the pastry and make it tough.

12. Heat the oven to Gas 8, 450F, 230C.

13. To Cook - bake 3 per person, brushed with the beaten egg to give a gloss for 12 minutes, or until golden. If cooking straight from the freezer allow an extra 2 minutes.

I usually serve them with a few dressed mixed leaves and Cucumber Raita: this is simply made by mixing some chopped cucumber and a little finely chopped onion into some plain thick yogurt.

Baked Parmesan Chicken Wings

A fiddle to do, but worth the effort as they are totally delicious. Good finger or barbecue food as you can hold them by their drumstick, without getting messy.

INGREDIENTS:

2 lbs(1 kilo) Chicken Wings, with the wing tip section removed at the joint

10 fl.oz(300ml) Plain Yogurt

Juice of 2 Lemons, sieved

1 tablespoon(15ml) Dijon Mustard

3 cloves of Garlic, peeled and finely chopped

$^1/_2$ teaspoon each of Dried Sage and Dried Oregano

1 pint Dried Breadcrumbs

$^1/_2$ pint of grated Parmesan

$^1/_2$ teaspoon of Cayenne Pepper

Half a teaspoon(3ml) Salt and plenty of freshly ground Black Pepper

4 oz(120g) Butter.

METHOD:

1. Cut the wings into 2 pieces at the joint.
2. With a small sharp knife scrap the meat from one end to the other, to give the appearance of a baby chicken drumstick.
3. Put the wings in a stainless steel or glass bowl with the yogurt, garlic, lemon juice, mustard, herbs and salt and pepper. Mix well so the meat is well covered.
4. Marinate for at least 2 hours at room temperature, or better still overnight in the fridge.
5. Combine the breadcrumbs with the parmesan and cayenne.
6. Heat the oven to Gas 6,400F,200C. Remove the wing pieces from their marinade and cover with the breadcrumb mixture - arrange the wings on a baking tray, in such a way that they are not touching.
7. Melt the butter and drizzle it over the wings.
8. Bake in the pre-heated oven for 30 minutes or until golden - the smell will be fantastic! Cool before removing carefully from baking tray.

* Can be prepared ahead up to this point. They can be eaten cold or re-heated.

Good by themselves or with an Aioli or Remoulade dip (q.v.)

Warm Gateau of Chicken or Duck Livers

If you have been saving livers from your poultry, in the deep freeze, this is an excellent way to use them, while impressing your friends at the same time.

They need a sauce to accompany them and both White Wine and Spring Onion Sauce or Warm Tomato Coulis (q.v.) fit the bill well.

These little mousses can be made the day before and gently re-heated in a steamer or microwave - they will however lose a little of their wobble!

EQUIPMENT:

Food Processor or liquidizer. Four to six ramekins (depending on size) or similar oven-proof containers. Tin foil squares to cover them.

INGREDIENTS:

4 oz(120g) Chicken or Duck Livers, carefully washed and with any sinews removed.

1 small clove of Garlic, peeled

2 teaspoons(2 × 5ml) Flour

2 × No.3 Eggs

2 × No.3 Egg Yolks (freeze the whites for use another time)

2 fl.oz(60ml) Double Cream

8 fl.oz(230ml) Milk

A few grates from a Nutmeg

A little Salt and freshly ground Black Pepper

A little soft butter for lining the ramekins.

METHOD:

1. Lightly butter the ramekins and set aside.

2. Set the oven to Gas 4, 350F, 180C.

3. Puree the livers with the garlic in a food processor or blender. Pour them into a big bowl or saucepan (so you can stir them vigorously without splashing)

4. Beat in the flour with a wooden spoon; followed by the eggs, egg yolks, cream, milk and seasonings.

5. Work this mixture through a sieve.

6. Pour the uncooked mousse into your prepared ramekins; don't fill them more than ³/₄ full - even if you have mixture left over - as the level will rise.

7. Cover each dish loosely with tin foil, to stop the tops browning.

* Can be prepared ahead up to this point - keep in the fridge until needed.

8. Put the moulds in a roasting tray and cook in the pre-heated oven for 30 minutes.

9. Remove from the oven. The mixture should have risen and be slightly coming away from the sides of the ramekins. A knife inserted into the middle will also come out clean. If unsure cook for a further few minutes.

To serve - leave to rest at room tempeature for 2-3 minutes (the mousses will settle back slightly into their moulds). Run a knife around the sides of the moulds and turn upside-down on to individual serving plates.

Cover with your chosen sauce.

Duck Terrine

This delicious terrine requires very little skill to prepare; it must, however, be started 36 hours ahead for the flavour to mature.

The preparation, in terms of man hours, is not long; but to develop it's full flavour it needs to marinate before cooking and to cool and set for at least 8 hours afterwards.

Once cooked it will continue to improve for 2-3 days; and can be stored in the fridge for up to 10 days with no adverse effects.

It is particularly delicious served with Onion Marmalade and Sweet and Sour Prunes (q.v.)

EQUIPMENT:

Food processor; a terrine capable of holding 2.5 pints(1.4l) of water or 2 smaller ovenproof bowls - see instuctions below.

INGREDIENTS (FOR 10-12 GOOD SLICES)

1 × 5lb(2.25kilo) Fresh oven-ready Duck

¼pint(140ml) Cognac or Armagnac

¼pint(140ml) Sercial Madeira or Dry Sherry

2 tablespoons(2 × 15ml) Sunflower Oil

1lb(454g) Unsmoked Streaky Bacon, with the rind removed

½lb(225g) unsalted fresh Pork Belly, with the rind and small bones removed - then cut into cubes

½lb(225g) Chicken Livers, drained; and the liver from your duck

2 big cloves of garlic, peeled and finely chopped

2 Bay Leaves

2 big pinches of dried thyme

1 × No.3 Egg

Salt and freshly ground black pepper

METHOD:

At least 36 hours, preferably more, before the terrine is to be served -

1. Remove the bag of giblets from the duck; save the liver from these, and throw the rest away.

2. Remove all the meat, including the fat and skin, from the duck; being careful to take out all the small bones. This is a very easy process and should'nt take more than 10 minutes.

3. Cut this meat into ½inch(1 cm) pieces and put it into a big glass or stainless steel bowl.

4. Add the chopped belly pork, Cognac, Madeira, garlic and herbs. Allow to marinate for a minimum of 4 hours at room temperature, or overnight in fridge if you have time.

5. Line your chosen terrine or ovenproof dish with the streaky bacon and set aside a few slices to cover the top. Any left over pieces should be chopped and added to your marinade mixture.
If you have to use 2 smaller terrines, don't despair - follow the instructions in the same way, but reduce the total cooking time by 30 minutes.

6. Drain the meat, reserving the marinade.

7. Heat the oil, over a medium heat, in a big saucepan and fry the meat together with the herbs and chicken/duck livers until they are brown ; stirring occasionally.

8. Allow the mixture to cool, then remove the bay leaves. Heat the oven to Gas 3, 325F, 160C.

9. Chop the mixture in a food processor until coursely chopped, but not over smooth. Add the egg, the reserved marinade, $^1/_2$ teaspoon(2ml) salt and a generous amount of freshly ground pepper and quickly process again.

10. Carefully pour the mixture into your prepared terrine, being careful not to disturb the bacon. Cover the top with the reserved bacon rashers.

11. Cover the container with tin foil, loosely sealing the edges.

12. Place in a roasting tin to catch any fat and cook for 1 hour 40 minutes in the pre-heated oven.

13. Cool slightly, then remove the foil and replace any fat and liquid that has leaked into the roasting tin.

14. Put the terrine complete with surrounding tin in the fridge and carefully balance some tins on top, to act as compressing weights.

15. Leave to set for at least 8 hours.

Serve cut into slices.

Individual Hot Leek and Bacon Tarts

This is a very good, but quite filling, starter - which, if dressed up with a salad would be ideal for a light lunch.

As an alternative you can offer 'Petits pots aux Poireax' which is the same recipe as below, but served in a ramekin instead of the pastry tart, and a good idea if your main course is a fairly substantial one.

EQUIPMENT:
4 small tart tins, loose-bottomed if possible.

INGREDIENTS FOR 4:
Half a batch of Garlic and Sherry (q.v.)

1 lb(450g) Leeks, with the root and the dark green top removed

3 oz(90g) of Unsmoked Streaky Bacon. with the rind removed

8 fl. oz(230ml) Single Cream

2 oz(60g) Freshly grated Parmesan

1 × No.2 or 2 No.4 Egg Yolks

1 oz(30g) Butter

Salt and freshly ground Pepper.

METHOD:
1. Slice the leeks into rings about $^1/_8$in(30mm) thick.

2. *Blanch* them in unsalted water for 3 minutes, strain and *refresh* under very cold running water. Shake, then squeeze them dry.

3. Cut the bacon into $^1/_2$in(1cm) pieces and fry over a medium heat for 2 - 3 minutes, remove the bacon squeezing out any surplus fat (which should be kept in the fridge for your next fry-up) and set aside.

4. Mix together the leeks (loosening them up a little), bacon, egg yolk, a little salt and freshly ground pepper, plus half the cheese - chill until required.

5. Prepare the tarts as directed in the recipe for Warm Tart of Rainbow Trout and Spring Onions (q.v.), baking them *blind* as directed.

* Can be prepared in advance to this stage.

6. Heat the oven to Gas 6, 400F, 200C.

7. Fill the tarts (which should still be in their tins) with the leek mixture, being careful not to spill any - if it overflows the tarts can become stuck in their tins.

8. Sprinkle with the remaining cheese and dot with butter.

9. Bake for 15 minutes.

To serve: allow to cool slightly, then remove the tarts from their tins. A little salad decoration sets them off well.

....*AND FOR RAMEKINS:*

Ignore the directions concerning pastry and at stage 7 share the mixture between the ramekins (there may be a little left over). Cook as for tarts.

Fried Fish Fillets in Gremolata Crumbs

Any white fish fillets will do, but very fresh plaice (a much underrated fish) are truly excellent. The garlic is in no way overpowering.

The crumbs, which are also the traditional accompaniment to Osso Buco, can be prepared and the fish breaded hours before needed.

INGREDIENTS FOR 4:

Your chosen Fish Fillets

8 tablespoons(8 × 15ml) freshly chopped Parsley

4 big cloves of Garlic, peeled and chopped

The freshly grated zest of 2 Lemons

4 oz(115g) fine dry Breadcrumbs: you can easily make these yourself with liquidized stale bread, gently baked in the oven until golden.

A plate of Flour, seasoned with Salt and freshly ground Pepper

2 whole Eggs, beaten together with a little salt to break down the albumin

2 additional Lemons, cut into thick wedges - or, if you are eating privately, you can use the lemons stiped of their zest.

Either clean oil in a fryer, or 2 tablespoons of Sunflower or Groundnut Oil

EQUIPMENT:

A deep fryer (optional)

METHOD:

1. Dip the fillets in the seasoned flour, then in the egg mixture, before coating well with breadcrumbs. Shake off any excess crumbs.

2. Leave on a tray in the fridge to firm-up until needed.

* Can be prepared ahead up to this point.

3. If deep frying, heat the oil to 325F, 160C. If shallow frying heat half the oil in a wide frying pan - as it will probably be easier to fry your fish in two batches.

4. If deep frying, fry until the fish floats and is golden - turning once.

5. If shallow frying, cook until golden - don't be tempted to add the fish to your pan until the oil is hot, or it will stew and absorb too much oil.

Serve with homemade Remoulade Sauce (q.v.).

Frying Fish Fillets

This simple technique works with fish fillets of all types (discounting squid and octopus that don't look like fish).

Unlike meat, which should never be salted before cooking, fish really benefits from this. So sprinkle on a little just before frying.

Have your fillets, whether plaice, sole, brill or cod cut to size and skinned ready in the fridge; and have your sauce or lemon wedges at the ready at room temperature (don't cut the lemon too early, or it will form an unattractive dry skin: also don't give your guests silly little slices that are impossible to squeeze - except over your clothes).

RELAX WITH YOUR GUESTS.

1. When ready to eat, melt a little good unsalted butter over a low to medium heat, in a wide pan.

2. When it starts to sizzle add your fillets, note their shiny opaque texture and firmness with no spring - this will change. A Fillet of plaice will need turning after 90 seconds, a 1 in(2.5cm) piece of cod or brill after about 3 minutes. After this time the colour will have changed to brilliant white (or pale pink for salmon) and the fish will have a spring to the touch.

3. When cooked a sharp knife will meet with no resistance.

Under-cook if unsure, your fish (like an egg) will continue to cook a little even when removed from the heat.

If serving simply with lemon, *deglaze* with a squeeze of lemon juice and an extra knob of butter to loosen all the goodies attached to the bottom of the pan and use this as a delicious sauce. Chips (q.v.), if good, are an excellent if unfashionable accompaniment: or serve with Caramelized Tomato Sauce (q.v.) or one of the variations of Fish Sauce Base listed below.

Crisping Fish Skin

Salmon steaks, Sea-Bass steaks (carefully de-scaled) and Whole Trout are delicious grilled with the skin on.

With fish steaks, put under a very hot grill - skin side up and cook for 5 to 8 minutes, depending on thickness: a light sprinkling of salt encourages the skin to crisp. The skinless side will cook in the reflected heat, so there's no need to turn the fish over. Rest the steaks on your chosen sauce, or serve simply with lemon.

Whole trout can be grilled in the same way, although they will need turning over after about 3 minutes; these are particularly good with a heavy sprinkling of sea salt and a light dusting of paprika before grilling.

Garlic Mashed Potato (q.v.) is an excellent accompaniment.

Fish Sauce Base

A sauce in it's own right (when it could be called Noilly Prat Sauce); also an excellent base for added chopped chives, chopped sorrel, shredded watercress or even lumpfish caviar (on no account add any extra salt with this).

INGREDIENTS: FOR 1 PINT(567ML)

10 fl.oz(300ml) Fish Stock (q.v.)

3 fl.oz(90ml) Noilly Prat (Dry Martini will not do)

2 fl.oz(70ml) Dry White Wine

4 oz(120g) Shallots, skinned and finely chopped

4 oz(120g) chopped Leek

18 fl.oz(500ml) Double Cream

2 fl.oz(60ml) Sauternes (optional, but adds to the sauces character)

1 teaspoon(5ml) Cornflour, dissolved in 1 tablespoon(15ml) cold water

2 oz(56g) Butter

Salt and Pepper, to taste.

METHOD:

1. Put the fish stock, Noilly Prat, white wine, leeks and shallots into a stainless steel pan, then *reduce* by half.

2. Add the cream, Sauterne if using and the dissolved cornflour.

3. Bring to the boil, simmer for 2 minutes, then whisk in the cold butter, until you have a smooth mixture and the sauce has slightly thickened.

4. Check the seasoning, then sieve into a clean container.

* Can be prepared ahead up to this point. If keeping , rub the surface of the sauce with a lump of butter, to stop a skin forming.

Just before serving add your chives, sorrel or watercress to the heated sauce; they will maintain their fresh colour.

Grilled Mackerel

A very underrated fish, possibly only neglected because it's so cheap. To avoid any lingering fishy smells the next time you use the grill, it is important to loosely line the grill with a tin foil base. This will also trap the delicious juices.

INGREDIENTS FOR 4:

4 Fresh Mackerel (about 6 oz(170g) each, cleaned and headed by your fishmonger

4 slices of Lemon

4 sprigs of Rosemary (optional)

Salt and freshly ground Pepper.

EQUIPMENT:

A baking tray, or similar, that fits under your grill - loosely lined with tin foil.

METHOD:

1. Wash the fish inside and out, then pat the fish dry with kitchen towel. Season inside and out with salt and pepper and insert a lemon slice and a sprig of rosemary (if using) into each cavity. Make 3 or 4 deep cuts on each side of the fish.

2. Prepare your grill tray with tin foil and heat the grill, giving it time to get really hot.

3. Grill the fish for 3 minutes on each side on your prepared tray, or until a small sharp knife comes out clean when inserted into the thickest part of the fish.

VARIATIONS:

Grilled Mackerel with Pesto

1. Wash and season and slash the fish, as described above.

2. Put a teaspoon(5ml) of Pesto Sauce (q.v.) into each slash on one side of the fish.

3. Grill this side for 3 minutes, then repeat the performance on the other side of the fish. Use a foil lining tray, as described above.

4. Any juices in the foil base should be poured over the fish when serving.

Grilled Mackerel with Orange Mustard

INGREDIENTS FOR STUFFING 4 FISH:

2 big Oranges with good skins

4 tablespoons(4 × 15ml) Dijon Mustard.

METHOD:

1. Wash, season and slash the fish, as directed under Grilled Mackerel.

2. Grate the orange zest into the mustard, then add the sieved juice from 1 orange.

3. Proceed as for Mackerel with Pesto, using the mustard as stuffing.

Serve with the juices poured over.

Trout with Pernod Sauce

The flavour of anise combines beautifully with fish, particularly trout which is in no way overpowered.

This dish can be reheated, but as it only takes a few minutes, I suggest that you have everything else ready and cook the fish freshly.

EQUIPMENT:

A wide frying pan.

INGREDIENTS FOR 4:

4 Fresh Rainbow Trout (about 8 oz/230g each), gutted by your fishmonger - the heads removed if you prefer (they may fit in your pan better like this)

1 small Onion (about 2 oz/60g), peeled and chopped

1 big or 2 medium cloves of Garlic, peeled and finely chopped

4 oz(120g) Mushrooms, sliced

3 oz(90g) Butter

2 fl.oz(60ml) Pernod or Ricard

12 fl.oz(300ml) Double Cream: use a little more if you are planning to re-heat the dish

A little Salt and freshly ground Pepper.

METHOD:

1. Lightly season the trout, inside and out, with salt and pepper. Melt 2 oz(60g) of the butter in the frying pan over a medium heat.

2. When it starts to sizzle add the chopped onion and garlic, lower the heat and *sweat* until soft.

3. Increase the heat to medium again and add the trout, gently shaking to stop them sticking.

4. Fry for about 5 minutes, then carefully turn the fish over - trying to keep the skin intact.

5. Add the remaining butter and the mushroom slices and cook for a further 3 minutes, turning the mushrooms over to ensure they cook.

6. Add the Pernod and let it bubble for a minute - don't be alarmed if it flares up, but be careful of your eyelashes!

7. Add the cream, plus a little more salt and pepper and gently swill the pan around to mix the ingredients.

Serve when the cream starts to bubble.

Penne with Fresh Salmon

Quick and easy to assemble, this is a good way of using up any fish you might have in the freezer: although the salmon mentioned is ideal. Serve with some good French bread and a salad.

INGREDIENTS FOR 4:

500g packet of Dried Penne; other pasta types can be substituted, but the way the penne quills hold the sauce makes them ideal

12 oz(340g) of uncooked Fresh Salmon Steaks, skinned by your fishmonger

1 oz(30g) Butter

1 tablespoon(15ml) Chopped Shallots or Spring Onions - include most of the green stalks

1 Leek, washed and chopped

1 medium clove of Garlic, peeled and chopped

5 fl.oz(140ml) Fish Stock or a quarter of a Fish Stock cube dissolved in water

5 fl.oz(140ml) Dry White Wine

1 pint(550ml) Double Cream

1 tablespoon(15ml) Fresh Dill

1 tablespoon(15ml) Fresh Chives

8 Fresh Basil Leaves

Salt and freshly ground Pepper

The juice of half a Lemon, sieved

1 50g (the smallest) jar of Lumpfish Caviar (optional)

METHOD:

Make the sauce first -

1. Melt the butter in a deep frying pan or wide based saucepan and *sweat* the shallots, garlic and leeks until transparent.

2. Add the salmon and gently fry for 3 minutes on each side; remove the fish to a plate to cool.

3. Add the wine to the pan and *deglaze;* pour in the fish stock and increase the heat until the liquid bubbles. *Reduce* by half.

4. Lower the heat and add the cream, stirring to mix well in.

5. Cut the salmon into 1 in(2.5cm) cubes and add to the sauce.

6. Add a little Salt (a bit more if you are not using caviar) and plenty of freshly ground pepper, then mix in the lemon juice.

* Can be prepared ahead up to this point.

7. Cook the pasta as directed on the packet, drain and *refresh* under cold water to wash out any surplus starch.

8. When completely free of water add to the sauce and heat gently.

9. Mix the fresh herbs in 1 minute before serving.

Serve each helping with a heaped teaspoonful(8ml) of lumpfish caviar piled in the centre.

Salmon en Papillote

I have given this recipe for salmon, but a steak of any firm fish is just as successful: Brill and Turbot spring to mind, but rolled up Dover Sole fillets or Monkfish medallions would be equally successful. If rolling up sole fillets, or the fillets of any fish for that matter; having removed the skin, make a few shallow cuts on this side and roll them so this becomes the inside. This way they are less likely to unroll. A cocktail stick is a useful add for some recipes, but if used here might puncture the parcel.

For thin fillets reduce the oven time to 10 minutes and cut out the preliminary sealing.

INGREDIENTS FOR 4:

4 × 6oz(170g) Salmon fillets, skinned

2 oz(60g) Butter

2 fl.oz(60ml) Noilly Prat - no other vermouth combines so well with fish

16 fl.oz(450ml) Double Cream

1 big Carrot, peeled

2 sticks of Celery, washed

1 big Leek, carefully washed - then the root and dark green sections removed (the hot green section can be used for stock)

Half a small Fennel bulb (optional)

A sprig of Fresh Tarragon or a small pinch of dried

Salt and freshly ground Pepper

The juice of half a Lemon, sieved.

EQUIPMENT:

10 in(25cm) squares of good tin foil or greaseproof paper.

METHOD:

1. Cut the vegetables into *julienne strips.*

2. Melt half the butter in a wide saucepan or frying pan and gently *sweat* the vegetable pieces for 3 minutes, adding the tarragon leaves and a little salt and pepper for the final minute. Mix well and transfer to a side dish, leaving the juices in the pan.

3. Add the remaining butter to the pan and increase the heat to medium.

4. Sprinkle the fish steaks with a little salt and pepper on both sides, then seal them by frying for 1 minute on each side. Remove them from the pan, so that they stop cooking instantly.

5. Add the Noilly Prat to the pan and *deglaze* any goodies; then mix in the cream and cook until it bubbles. Remove from the heat.

6. Assemble your parcels by sharing out the ingredients, putting just a few vegrtables strips underneath the fish, but most on top.

7. Loosely secure the parcels, allowing plenty of air space inside.

* Can be prepared ahead up to this point and kept at room temperature for a few hours or in the fridge if overnight.

8. Heat the oven to Gas 6, 400F, 200C.

9. Put your parcels, on a baking tray, at the top of the oven for 15 minutes.

10. Remove.

To serve, either unwrap in the kitchen or produce the parcels at the table allowing your guests to unwrap their own.

Serve with simple vegetables and perhaps new potatoes.

Cassoulet

This luxurious form of baked beans takes a few days of gentle and trouble free preparation, but will leave you free to entertain your guests, as it can be produced straight from the oven.

There is still fierce rivalry in south-west France as to which town produces the true Cassoulet.

The recipe given here has been adapted to use ingredients likely to be at hand - but is none the less delicious.

Interestingly enough, the now more or less standard dried haricots are not native to France - being like tomatoes and potatoes American immigrants. A similar dish was made before their arrival using the indigenous feves or broad beans.

These still make a pleasant change (9lbs of fresh pods will produce the quantity of beans for this dish) the beans should be introduced at stage 7 of the cooking process.

On no account be tempted to try butter beans, as they will simply fall to bits.

There are 3 distinct processes. The beans and meats are partly cooked separately to start with. Both are then combined at the final stage.

A simple salad would be the ideal accompaniment.

EQUIPMENT:

A big casserole with a tight-fitting lid, or if wanting to present the dish at the table, a traditional earthenware Cassole.

INGREDIENTS FOR 8 - 10:

For the beans -

2 lb(900g) dried White Haricot Beans, soaked overnight in cold water

1 Carrot, peeled and roughly chopped

1 big Onion, peeled and stuck with 4 cloves

4 cloves of Garlic, peeled and left whole

1 teaspoon(5ml) Herbes de Provence.

For the meat ragout -

6 jointed legs of Duck Confit (q.v.), or Roast Duck Legs (again jointed)

2 tablespoons(2 × 15ml) Duck Fat or Lard

1 Shoulder of Lamb, cut into 1 in(2.5cm) cubes and any surplus fat removed

1 lb(450g) Cubed Pork, shoulder or loin meat is ideal

1 lb(450g) air-dried sausage, cut into pieces: although not authentic, I find Polish Kabanos excellent and they hold together well

1 400g tin of Chopped Tomatoes

2 big Onions, peeled and chopped

4 cloves of Garlic, peeled and chopped

10 fl.oz(280ml) Dry White Wine

2 pints(900ml) Weak Chicken Stock - made with 1 stockcube

Salt and freshly ground Black Pepper

To finish -

4 oz(120g) Fresh White Breadcrumbs - optional.

1 teaspoon(5ml) Herbes de Provence.

METHOD:

1. First cook the beans - put them in a big saucepan with their accompanying ingredients, cover with water and simmer for 2 hours.

2. Drain the beans and set aside, but keep their cooking liquid.

3. The Meat Ragout - Set the oven to Gas 2, 300F, 150C. Heat the duck fat or lard in a deep frying pan and soften the onions and garlic for 5 minutes. Transfer these to your big casserole, using a perforated spoon so you leave as much fat behind as possible.

4. Increase the flame, then seal the pork and lamb, in batches; and add to the casserole with any remaining fat.

5. Add the stock, wine, herbs and tomatoes plus a little salt and pepper and mix well in.

6. Bring this mixture to simmering point, cover and cook in the oven for 2 hours. Leave the oven on, but remove the casserole.

7. Add the drained beans and the duck and sausage pieces.

8. Mix until it is all well combined.

9. Make sure that the liquid comes to the top of the mixture; so top-up with some bean water if necessary.

10. Return to the oven and cook, covered for a further hour. Remove from the oven. Check the seasonings.

* Can be prepared ahead up to this point; and will, in fact, improve as the flavours amalgamate. If keeping overnight, make sure that the mixture is moist before reheating (so topping-up with a little water might be necessary), as the beans will continue to absorb liquid.

When serving, heat, uncovered, in a medium oven (Gas 5, 375F, 190C) sprinkled with the fresh breadcrumbs, if using (the crumbs should be golden and crisp). Or microwave individually, if prefered.

Calf's Liver with Onions and Lemon

This Venetian style dish can be prepared with lambs liver if eating veal is a moral problem. Preparations can leave you with only 2 or 3 minutes work in the kitchen to finish finish off the dish.

INGREDIENTS FOR 4:

1.5 lb(700g) Calf's Liver (ask your butcher to slice this very thinly for you: if you have to do this yourself, chill it in the deep freeze first for an hour, to firm it up

2 big Onions, peeled, cut in half, then thinly sliced

2 tablespoons(2 × 15ml) good Olive Oil

3 oz(90g) Butter

3 tablespoons(3 × 15ml) White Wine Vinegar

2 tablespoons(2 × 15ml) chopped fresh Parsley

1 pinch dried Thyme

Salt, a few grates of Nutmeg and some freshly ground Pepper

To serve; 1 Lemon divided into quarters.

METHOD:

1. Put the olive oil and onions into a stainless steel saucepan and cook over a low heat for about 15 minutes, stirring occasionally, until the onions are soft.

2. Add the vinegar and continue cooking until it has reduced by half. Set aside.

* The dish can be prepared up to this stage.

3. You must now work quickly (as the liver needs very little cooking), so have vegetables completely ready. In a big frying pan, melt the butter over a moderate heat until it foams.

4. Turn up the heat, then add the liver and fry for about one minute on each side until sealed and golden.

5. Add the onion mixture, the parsley, thyme, nutmeg, salt and pepper.

6. Combine the mixture well.

Serve with lemon wedges and the juices poured over.

Medallions of Venison with a Poached Pear and Cassis Sauce

An impressive looking dish, which is easy to prepare; the spade work can be completed the day before if necessary - in fact will be better for it - just leaving you to fry the meat at the last minute.

Venison is freely available from supermarkets all the year round: if you can't find a boned saddle (which looks like a sausage and cuts into medallions) a steak cut into individual squares would suffice. In either case, treat the meat as you would a steak - although cooking well-done would leave it rather dry.

INGREDIENTS FOR 4:

2 Comice Pears, slightly on the hard side: peeled, cored and carefully cut into halfs

5 fl.oz(140ml) Heavy Red Wine

3 lb(1.4 kilos) piece of Saddle of Venison, boned-out by your butcher - or an equivalent, see introduction

2 oz(60g) Butter

1 clove of Garlic, peeled and cut in half

8 fl.oz(200ml) Cheap Port

1 Bay Leaf

2 tablespoons(2 × 15ml) Creme de Cassis or Blackcurrant cordial

1 dessertspoon(10ml) Tomato Puree

Salt and freshly ground Black Pepper.

EQUIPMENT:

A stainless steel saucepan big enough to arrange the pears in flat.

METHOD:

1. Poach the pears in the red wine for 15 minutes, adding a top-up of just enough water to cover them completely. Leave to cool in the liquid.

2. Cut the venison into your desired shape, about 1 in(2.5cm) thick is ideal. Then wipe the meat with the cut garlic clove and season with a little pepper. *Marinate* in port, with the bay leaf, for a minimum of 2 hours, overnight if prefered.

* Can be prepared ahead up to this point.

3. Melt half the butter in a wide frying pan over a medium heat, when it sizzles, seal the venison for 1 minute on each side, then remove from the pan and keep to one side.

4. *Deglaze* with the port *marinade*, add the cassis, tomato puree and season with a little salt and pepper. *Reduce* the sauce until it thickens slightly.

5. While the sauce is bubbling, arrange a pear half - flat side down - on each plate.

6. Slice thinly, from the thick end, leaving the fruit attached at the other: then gently press down to form a fan shape. Heat in the oven or microwave for a few seconds.

7. Whisk the remaining butter into your sauce and immerse the meat to heat through.

Serve nicely arranged, with any vegetables in separate bowls, so as not to spoil the effect.

Roast Leg of Lamb with Flageolets

Easy to prepare. Apart from occasional basteing, which is very important, this dish only needs attention for the last 10 minutes - allowing you to talk to your guests. If you're worried about carving, have your leg of lamb boned and rolled; you will, however, lose a little flavour that is always produced by cooking meat on the bone. Either way carving can be carried out at the table, as it's part of the social occasion.

Dauphinoise Potatoes (q.v.) are delicious with this dish - these can either be prepared in advance and re-heated, or cooked at the same time on a low shelf of the oven.

INGREDIENTS FOR A GENEROUS 6:

1 Leg of Lamb, weighing about 6 lb(2.7 kg)

3 cloves of garlic, peeled and cut into long slivers

2 sprigs of fresh Rosemary, or 2 teaspoons(2 × 5ml) dried

10 fl.oz(300ml) Dry White Wine

1 tablespoon(15ml) Olive Oil

Freshly ground Pepper

10 fl.oz Water

1 batch of Flageolets, prepared as below.

METHOD:

1. Heat the oven to Gas 9, 475F, 250C and work out your cooking time. This will be 12 minutes per lb. for rare meat, 16 for medium and 20 for well done.

2. Cut off any excess fat from the lamb, then make little slits all over it and insert the garlic slivers and some of the rosemary needles in these.

3. Place the meat in a roasting tray and sprinkle it generously with pepper, then rub it with the olive oil - no salt at this stage, as it draws moisture out of the meat.

4. Put the remaining rosemary sprigs in the tray and pour the wine around the joint.

5. Roast for 15 minutes at the above temperature, then reduce the oven to Gas 6, 400F, 200C for the remainder of the cooking time.

6. Baste the meat every 10 minutes, not leaving the oven door open for longer than necessary; add the water to the roasting tray about half way through cooking.

7. When ready, turn off the oven, remove the meat and pour off the juices into a glass or plastic jug. Season the meat with a little salt, then return it to the oven, leaving the door slightly ajar, for a few minutes while you finish the sauce. This resting allows the sinews of the joint to relax and produces more tender meat.

8. The fat will quickly come to the surface of the juices and can be easily removed. Check the sauce for seasoning, it will need a little salt but probably no pepper.

9. Carve and serve, adding a little sauce to your bean mixture and passing the rest round in a jug.

Flageolets

To accompany lamb, or as a vegetable in their own right.

Flageolets are the bean pods from young haricots, if you grow them yourself you can use them fresh. Follow the instructions below, but only cook for 30 minutes.

If, like most of us, you have to rely on dried, buy them from a shop with a good turnover, or they can need soaking and cooking for ever.

In an emergency tinned beans are satisfactory (two 400g tins will produce a similar quantity), especially if improved with meat juices. But they will lack that something extra in the way of flavour.

These can be prepared ahead of time, kept in the fridge for 2 or 3 days, then re-heated.

EQUIPMENT:

Food Processor or Mouli-legume.

INGREDIENTS FOR A GENEROUS 6:

1 lb(450g) dried Flageolet Beans

1 big Onion, peeled and chopped

4 cloves of Garlic, peeled but left whole

1 Bay Leaf

1 sprig of fresh Rosemary, or a pinch of dried

Salt and freshly ground Pepper.

METHOD:

1. For dried beans, either soak them in plenty of cold water overnight; or if time is more pressing - bring them to the boil with enough water to cover them by 2 in.(5cm.), remove from the heat and allow them to soften for an hour. Drain, then proceed as if they had been soaked overnight.

2. Starting with drained beans, place in a big saucepan with the onion, garlic, herbs and enough water to cover by about 2 in.(5cm.).

3. Bring to the boil and *simmer* until the beans are tender, this will depend on the freshness of the pulses, but will be an hour or perhaps a little more.

4. Strain the water from the pan, keeping a little, fish out the visible herbs from the beans.

5. Liquidize about a quarter of the beans with as many of the garlic cloves as you can find and enough of the cooking liquid to make a puree. Stir back into the pan of beans.

6. Season with salt and freshly ground pepper.

Reheat when the lamb is ready, with a little of it's juices and a drop of water, if needed.

Moroccan Tagine of Lamb

This highly scented dish needs planning a day in advance for the best results; and will continue to improve for a few days. During the middle ages, dishes of this type were popular in England; the exotic flavourings being introduced by returning crusaders. A tagine is a traditional earthenware cooking pot. Serve this with steamed cous cous (see the packet for instructions), or Pilau Rice (q.v.). Preserved Lemons are the traditional accompaniment; I have adapted this to Lemon or Lime Pickle (q.v.).

EQUIPMENT:

A stainless steel or traditional earthenware ovenproof casserole, with a close-fitting lid: attractive if you wish to present it to the table.

INGREDIENTS FOR 6-8, DEPENDING ON SIZE OF LAMB LEG:

1 Boned leg of Lamb, with all the excess fat removed then cut into 2 oz(60g) cubes

Marinade ingredients -

2 teaspoons(2 × 5ml) Ground Ginger

1 big pinch of Saffron Strands, or a small packet of Powdered Saffron

1 teaspoon(5ml) Paprika

1 teaspoon(5ml) Ground Cumin

1 big Onion, peeled and chopped

2 big or 4 medium cloves of Garlic, peeled and chopped

1 oz(30g) Coriander Leaves, chopped

4 fl.oz(115ml) Olive Oil

To finish -

Salt and freshly ground Black Pepper

1 400/440g tin of Chick Peas, drained

1 tablespoon(15ml) Tomato Puree.

METHOD:

1. Place the lamb pieces in the casserole with the marinade ingredients and blend well together.

2. Leave to stand for a few hours, at room temperature, or overnight in the fridge.

3. Pre-heat the oven to Gas 2, 300F, 150C.

4. Cover the meat with water, cover with the lid, then cook in the oven for 2 hours.

5. Remove from the oven, season with salt and pepper, then add the tomato puree and drained chick peas - stir well.

6. Turn the oven up to Gas 3, 325F, 160C. Return the casserole to the oven, uncovered, and cook for a further 30 minutes or until the lamb is very tender.

* Can be prepared ahead up to this stage. If you have trimmed the meat carefully there should be very little surplus fat, only a little floating olive oil.

This helps to lubricate the meat, but can be easily removed as the dish cools a little, if preferred.

Chicken Bouillabaisse

A bastardization of the delicious, but time consuming, Provencal fish dish. Can be prepared well ahead of time, so you can relax when it's important.
Serve in bowls with Cheats Rouille (q.v.), a good salad and plenty of French bread.

EQUIPMENT:
Glass or stainless steel bowl, big enough to hold all ingredients; flameproof casserole.

INGREDIENTS FOR 4:
1 Free-range chicken, cut into 8 pieces (or the same number of chicken pieces) and the skinned removed

1 big pinch of Saffron Strands, or a small packet of Saffron Powder

A sherry glass (about 2 fl.oz/60ml) Pernod or Ricard

4 fl.oz(110ml) Good Olive Oil

1 big Onion, peeled, quartered, then thinly sliced

2 big, or 4 medium cloves of Garlic; peeled and chopped

1 head of Fennel, quartered then *blanched* for 1 minute, drained and *refreshed*

1 400g tin of Chopped Tomatoes

4 medium waxy-type Potatoes, peeled and cut into pieces of equal size (Desiree or big Cyprus/Egyptian potatoes such as Nicola's are ideal: floury potatoes will simply fall to bits)

1 tablespoon(15ml) freshly chopped Parsley

Salt and freshly ground Black Pepper.

METHOD:
1. Put the chicken pieces in the bowl, together with the Pernod, saffron and half the oil.

2. Season with freshly ground pepper; mix well together, then leave to marinate for a minimum of one hour at room temperature, or overnight in a fridge, turning the pieces over occasionally.

3. Heat the remaining oil in the casserole and gently fry the onions, *blanched* fennel and garlic until they are lightly golden; do not allow the vegetables to burn.

4. Add the tomatoes and cook gently for a further 5 minutes.

5. Add the chicken pieces, and their marinade to the casserole, sprinkle with the chopped parsley and add enough water to cover the chicken.

6. Bring the mixture to the boil, reduce the heat to maintain a simmer and cook for 10 minutes.

7. Add the potato pieces and season the dish with a little salt. Mix well together.

8. Continue to simmer, uncovered, for a further 20 minutes.

9. Remove the chicken and big vegetable pieces - keep these warm.

10. *Reduce* the remaining liquid by half, check the seasoning.

* Can be prepared ahead up to this point, then gently re-heated.

Serve in bowls and pass round a bowl of Cheats Rouille.

Coq au Vin

This classic dish from the Burgundy region has been badly misrepresented over the years: partly because of the sex of the bird - which more often than not is a Poularde; and partly because it is so seldom done justice.

Your Poularde au Vin will open your eyes to the deliciousness that spread it's popularity around the globe to start off with.

Pheasant or Guinea Fowl can be cooked in the same way. Each bird will provide 2 generous helpings, a cock pheasant three.

Although it is child's play to make, it will take you 3 days from start to finish. There are 3 distinct stages -

1. Marination

2. Cooking

3. Maturing and the removal of surplus fat

INGREDIENTS FOR 4:

For the marinade -

1 5lb(2.25 kilo) Free Range Chichen, divided into 8 pieces (your butcher will do this if you lack confidence)

1 big Onion, peeled and chopped

1 big Carrot, peeled and cut into small dice

4 Shallots, peeled and chopped or 1 Leek, washed and chopped

1 teaspoon(5ml) Herbes de Provence

1 Bay Leaf

2 big cloves of Garlic, peeled and chopped

20 Black Peppercorns, crushed (you can do this easily in a plastic bag)

1 bottle(75cl) full-bodied Red Wine

To cook the chicken -

1 tablespoons(2 × 15ml) Olive Oil

1 oz(30g) Butter

1 oz(30g) Plain White Flour, sieved

10 fl.oz(280ml) Hot Chicken Stock (use 1 stock cube, I find Knorr the best)

1 tablespoon(15ml) Creme de Cassis or Blackcurrant Juice (this accentuates the flavour of the wine)

1 tablespoon(15ml) Tarragon Vinegar

To finish -

8 oz(230g) Flat Mushrooms, cut into quarters

1 oz(30g) Butter

6 oz(170g) Unsmoked Streaky Bacon, with the rind removed and cut into 1 in.(2.5cm) pieces

16-20 baby (pickling type) Onions, peeled and left whole: if you leave the root intact, they are less likely to fall apart

A small glass (about 2ml) Cognac or Armagnac

A little Salt and probably no Pepper

1 tablespoon(15ml) chopped Parsley, to decorate.

METHOD:

1. Skin the chicken pieces and place in a stainless steel or glass container with the other marinade ingredients: refrigerate for about 10 hours, turning the pieces occasionally.

2. Drain the pieces of chicken, keeping the marinade, vegetables and peppercorns.

3. Pre- heat the oven to Gas 3, 350F, 180C.

4. Heat the olive oil and butter in a deep frying pan, over a fairly high flame.

5. Sear the purple chicken pieces, in batches, for 2 minutes on each side, to seal them and help keep in their flavour. Make sure that the pan re-heats properly in between each set.

6. Pile the chicken up, to one side, until they are all sealed.

7. Remove the pan from the heat and mix in the flour, making sure that you smooth out all the lumps with the back of a spoon.

8. Lower the flame and return the pan to the heat: then gradually add the marinade liquid and the vinegar to the roux, whisking gently to prevent any lumps forming as it thickens.

9. Transfer the chicken pieces to a casserole and add the thickened marinade and the reserved vegetables. If you are worried about any lumps, pass the sauce through a sieve. Add the hot stock and mix all together, making sure that the chicken and vegetables are covered.

10. Cover with a lid and cook in the oven for 55 minutes.

11. While the chicken is cooking, melt the remaining butter in the frying pan, over a medium heat.

12. Fry the baby onions until they are lightly brown (about 5 minutes), then add the bacon and seal. Finally add the mushrooms, turning them over gently until they are cooked.

13. Pour over the Cognac, then add this mixture to the cooked chicken and mix stir in.

14. Check the seasoning; you may need a little salt, but probably no pepper - remember that the bacon will continue to produce salt as the dish rests.

15. Return the caserole to the oven and cook for a further 15 minutes, covered and undisturbed.

16. Remove the casserole from the oven and leave in a cool corner overnight.

17. Skim any fat from the surface.

* The dish can be prepared ahead up to this point, but can be kept in the fridge for 3-4 days (indeed it will continue to improve). It can also be frozen for up to a month.

Pickled Pork Vindaloo

The description Vindaloo is generally misused; often just seeming to denote the hottest curry produced by a Indian restaurant. The dish, in fact, comes from a time when Goa was a Portuguese colony; the name being derived from their word for vinegar – an essential ingredient.

This preserve should be kept in a sterilized kilner type jar and will keep for many months in a fridge. Use as required as a side dish and to pep up bland curries.

Make sure that the meat is always completely sealed with fat.

EQUIPMENT:

A big flame-proof casserole, stainless steel if possible, with a close fitting lid. A 2 litre Preserving Jar, or several screw-top jam jars: *(see Lemon or Lime Pickle (q.v.) for the sterilizing method)*.

INGREDIENTS:

3lb(1.4 kilo) Fresh Belly Pork Rashers, with the rind removed

2 big Onions, peeled, then quartered and sliced

2 big, or 4 medium cloves of Garlic; peeled and chopped

5 fl.oz(140ml) Sunflower or Groundnut Oil

4oz(110g) Hot Curry Paste – this will produce a heat acceptable to all, so use more if preferred

A 400g tin of Chopped Tomatoes and their juices

10 fl.oz(280ml) Wine Vinegar

METHOD:

1. Cut the Pork into 2in(5cm) pieces.

2,. Over a medium heat, fry the onions and garlic until they soften – about 5 minutes.

3. Add the paste and mix well in.

4. Raise the heat, then add the pork pieces turning them around so they seal.

5. Add the tomatoes and vinegar and bring the mixture to the boil.

6. Remove from the heat, cover, and set aside for a few hours (or overnight if preferred) for the flavours to amalgamate.

7. Heat the oven to Gas 2, 300F, 150C. Bring the mixture to simmering point on the top of the cooker.

8. Then cook, covered, in the oven for 90 minutes.

9. Cool completely, then pot and keep, in covered jars, in a cool dark place.

Refrigerate once opened.

Sussex Braised Steak

A medieval recipe, which relies on the slow cooking method: so needs no attention.

As the meat retains it's shape, it won't occur to your guests that it is in fact casseroled - unless you chose to tell them!

INGREDIENTS FOR 4:
4 thick pieces of beef top rump or flank, shaped like a steak

1 big Onion, peeled and cut into rings

2 tablespoons(2 × 15ml) Flour

5 fl.oz(140ml) Port

5 fl.oz(140ml) Guinness

3 tablespoons(3 × 15ml) White Wine Vinegar

Salt and freshly ground Black Pepper.

EQUIPMENT:
A casserole with a tight-fitting lid, wide enough to take the meat lying flat.

METHOD:
1. Put the flour onto a big plate and season with plenty of black pepper - no salt at this stage. Mix the pepper well in. Heat the oven to Gas 1, 275F, 140C.
2. Coat the steaks with the flour, shaking off any excess.
3. Put the steaks in the casserole, so they are not overlapping; cover evenly with the onion rings.
4. Pour over the liquids and cover with the lid.
5. Cook in the oven for 3 hours. Add a little salt and serve.

Delicious!

Serve with Mashed Potatoes (q.v.).

Beef Olives Nicoise

This dish can be completed well ahead of time and carefully re-heated. Don't be frightened by the anchovies, they make a beautiful marriage with beef and you won't notice them. But you would notice their absence!

Equipment: A casserole with a tight-fitting lid. An ovenproof plate that neatly fits inside the casserole, this saves any fiddling about with string.

INGREDIENTS FOR 4:
8 slices of very thinly sliced beef (each slice to weigh about 3 oz/80g) : topside or silverside are ideal - your butcher will advice you

3 oz(90g) Unsmoked Streaky Bacon, de-rinded and cut into small pieces

4 Anchovy fillets, cut in half

2 oz(60g) Capers, drained

2 medium cloves of Garlic, peeled and chopped

4 hard-boiled Eggs, peeled and quartered

1 oz(30g) Fresh Parsley: washed, dried and chopped

Freshly ground Black Pepper and possibly a little Salt

10 fl.oz(280g) Heavy Red Wine

16 fl.oz(450g) Beef Stock (q.v.) or the same quantity of stock made with half a beef cube

1 tablespoon(15ml) Tomato Purée

METHOD:

1. Pre-heat the oven to Gas 3, 325F, 160C. Remove any excess fat from the meat, then gently beat out as thinly as possible under a sheet of cling film (this will save your kitchen walls from a bombardment of flying meat).

2. Place a slice of meat flat on a plate and place an egg quarter, a little garlic, half an anchovy fillet a teaspoon of capers, a little bacon and parsley on its centre. Add a generous grind of pepper.

3. Roll up the slice and place in the casserole.

4. Repeat this procedure with the other meat slices.

5. Wedge the rolls together to stop them unrolling, then cover with a plate to keep them in position.

6. Carefully add the wine, stock and tomato puree; plus any scraps of bacon etc. that you have left over.

7. Gently swirl the pan around to help to mix in the tomato puree - the cooking action will finish this process, so don't worry too much.

8. Cook the dish in the oven for 90 minutes.

Serve with Mashed Potatoes and Red Cabbage (q.v.).

Roast and Braised Rabbit with Mustard

Rabbit is slowly returning to popularity in this country, where it's association with Beatrix Potter has made us stupidly sentimental. Thank goodness other farmyard animals have'nt been so handicapped; a book on Florence the chicken or Benny the bull would seriously hamper our eating habits.

Rabbit is low in fat, so considered very healthy; but a drawback of this is that if it is overcooked it will become dry and uninteresting.

Like game birds, the legs take longer to cook than the body, so, in this recipe we will braise them a little longer than the saddle.

A rabbit provides a generous meal for two people, but not quite enough for three - but any leftovers re-heat well. The mustard is not overpowering, but enhances the delicate flavour of the meat.

If this seems like a long winded recipe, it isn't: because while your stock is reducing you can prepare most of the rest of the dish. The final trick is to add a little fresh mustard just before you bring the dish to the table.

INGREDIENTS FOR 4:

2 Farmed Rabbits, cut into big pieces by your butcher

2 oz(60g) Butter

About 2 oz(60g) Flour

3 Old Carrots, peeled and cut into small dice

3 Celery Stalks, washed and cut into small dice

1 Leek, carefully washed, then chopped

2 big Onions, peeled and chopped

2 big cloves of Garlic, peeled and chopped

1 tablespoon(15ml) Olive Oil

10 fl.oz(280ml) Dry White Wine

20 fl.oz(580ml Stock, prepared as below

A teaspoon(5ml) Herbes de Provence

2 dessertspoons(2 × 10ml) Dijon Mustard, to finish

5 fl.oz(140ml) Cream

Salt and freshly ground Pepper

Another tablespoon(15ml) Dijon Mustard

Freshly chopped Parsley, to decorate.

EQUIPMENT:
Flameproof casserole capable of holding all the ingredients.

METHOD:

1. Spread your rabbit pieces out, so you can see what you have.

2. Put the rear legs (meaty) and the saddle pieces on one side, the skinny front pieces on the other.

3. Put the skinny bits in a saucepan with half the onions, carrots, celery, garlic and all the Herbes de Provence.

4. Cover with 2 pint(1l.) water, bring to the boil and *simmer* for 90 minutes, pushing the rabbit pieces down to keep them below the liquid as they cook.

5. Drain, keeping the stock and throwing away the solids.

6. While the stock is reducing, put the flour on a dinner plate or roasting tray and season with plenty of salt and pepper: mix well together.

7. One by one, roll the meaty rabbit pieces in the seasoned flour - shaking off any excess, then putting them to one side. Any left over flour can be thrown away.

8. In the casserole, assemble half the butter, the remaining onion, celery, garlic and the leek; *sweat* for 5 minutes. Add the 2 dessertspoons of mustard, followed by the white wine: scraping the bottom of the pan to *deglaze*. Set aside.

9. Heat the oven to Gas 6, 400F, 200C.

10. In a separate frying pan, melt the remaining butter over a medium flame until it sizzles. Fry the rabbit pieces on all sides until they are sealed and are golden brown: as you are happy with them, take them out and put them in a roasting tin; adding any leftover juices to the vegetable casserole.

11. Pour the olive oil over the rabbit and roast for 10 minutes, turning them over half way through. Remove from the oven.

12. Put the rabbit legs (which as mentioned take longer to cook) in the casserole with the vegetable mixture, then add the reserved stock- allowing the saddle pieces to cool to one side. Bring the casserole to the boil and "simmer" for 15 minutes. Remove from the heat and allow to cool.

13. Remove the rabbit legs from the sauce and stack them up with the saddle meat.

14. *Reduce* the sauce by half, over a medium heat.

* The dish can be prepared ahead to this point.

15. When ready to serve, add the cream and lemon juice to the sauce and heat.

16. Put the rabbit pieces in the oven for 2 minutes.

17. Just before serving, mix the extra spoon of mustard into the sauce and test the seasoning. Combine the rabbit and sauce and sprinkle with fresh parsley.

Very good with Mashed Poatatoes (q.v.) to soak up the juices.

Vegetable Pot au Feu with Harissa

A man-sized meal to satisfy vegetarians and carnivores alike. The dish can be served as soup one day and as something more substantial the next, perhaps with Pilau Rice (q.v.). Determined meat eaters could have a side dish of fiery Pickled Pork Vindaloo (q.v.).

EQUIPMENT:
A big casserole, stainless steel if possible, capable of holding all the ingredients

INGREDIENTS FOR 6:
for the stock -

6 smallish Red Onions, trimmed but unpeeled

6 ordinary Onions, of a similar size, trimmed but unpeeled

6 big cloves of Garlic, peeled but left whole

5 pints(2.8l) Boiling Water

for the stew -

6 Old Carrots, peeled and trimmed

2 Celery Hearts, divided into quarters

3 big Leeks, cut across to make 6 pieces, carefully washed, or 6 small Leeks

1 Bouquet Garni, comprising of a teaspoon(5ml) Herbes de Provence and a Bay Leaf - wrapped in a little muslin parcel or held in a tea infuser

2 big cloves of Garlic, peeled and chopped

2 Cinnamon Sticks

A firm Cauliflower, divided into segments

6 oz(170g) stringless Kenya Beans, headed and tailed

6 small firm Courgettes, headed and tailed

2 Sweet Peppers, de-seeded and cut into 1in(2.5cm) pieces

8 oz(230g) frozen Peas

1 400g tin of Chopped Tomatoes

1 400/440g tin of Chick Peas, drained

2 teaspoons(2 × 5ml), or more, of Harissa (easily available from big supermarkets in small tins or jars)

Salt and freshly ground Pepper

METHOD:

1. Put the stock ingredients together with the boiling water. Return to the boil and *simmer* for 30 minutes.
2. Carefully fish out the solids with a perforated spoon and cool on a plate.
3. Add the carrots, celery, leeks, chopped garlic, bouquet garni and cinnamon to the water. Return the water to the boil and *simmer* for 5 minutes.
4. Add the cauliflower pieces and 5 minutes later the courgettes, peppers and chick peas.
5. While the vegetables are cooking, carefully peel the onions - add these with the garlic intact to the pan with the frozen peas. Cook for a further 5 minutes.
6. Taste for seasonings, adding as much salt and pepper as necessary.
7. Add the harissa and gently mix well in. Taste again, adding more harissa if you want more fire.
* Can be prepared up to this point and re-heated. If planning this, be careful not to overcook the vegetables.

Carrot and Parmesan Filo Parcel

You would'nt believe carrots could taste so good!
These parcels can be prepared a day in advance and finished at the last moment.

INGREDIENTS FOR 4:

1 lb(450g) Old Carrots, peeled
1 medium Onion, peeled
1 big or 2 medium cloves of Garlic, peeled
6 oz(170g) Butter
4 oz(110g) grated fresh Parmesan - please don't be tempted to use dried
4 oz(110g) Curd Cheese, or similar
A big pinch of dried Thyme
Salt and freshly ground Pepper
4 sheets of Filo Pastry - I find frozen filo very good; you can partially thaw, carefully remove what you need, then re-freeze the remainder
1 Egg, lightly beaten.

METHOD:

1. Finely chop the onion, carrots and garlic.
2. Melt 1 oz(30g) of the butter and gently *sweat* the vegetables in it for 3-4 minutes. Allow to cool slightly.
3. Add half the grated parmesan, the curd cheese, thyme and salt and pepper; mix well. Allow to cool, if time is available.
4. Melt the remaining butter in a small saucepan.
5. Spread out a filo pastry sheet. Paint one half of it with some melted butter, sprinkle a little parmesan on the buttered half. Then fold the un-buttered half over to form a rectangle.
6. Spread one quarter of the carrot mixture down the middle of pastry, leaving good margins all around.
7. Fold the pastry over on all sides to make a parcel, using a little melted butter as glue.
* Can be prepared ahead up to this point; keep on a floured tray in the fridge.
8. When ready to cook, heat oven to Gas 7, 425F, 220C.
9. When hot, glaze the parcel top with a little beaten egg, then bake in the oven for 15 minutes or until the pastry is crisp.
Serve with Hollandaise Sauce (q.v.).

Simple Courgettes or Mange Touts

A way of quickly cooking these vegetables and preserving all their flavour.

EQUIPMENT:
A wide-based stainless steel pan, with a close fitting lid.

INGREDIENTS FOR 4:

1 lb(454g) Small Firm Courgettes (anything too big will have large seeds and have watery tendencies) or slightly 12 oz(340g) Mange Tout

3 tablespoons(3 × 15ml) Good Olive Oil

1 small clove of Garlic, finely chopped

A tiny squeeze of Lemon Juice

Salt and freshly ground Black Pepper.

METHOD:

1. Head and tail the courgettes; if very small leave them whole, if larger cut in half lengthways. For mange tout, head and tail - being careful to remove the string on the pea-side of the pods.

2. Put the olive oil and chopped garlic in the saucepan over a medium heat.

3. Add the vegetables, making sure they have the maximum possible contact with the base of the pan. Seal with the lid.

4. Shake and cook for 2 minutes.

5. Season with a little salt and pepper, plus the merest squeeze of lemon juice.

*Can be cooked a few hours in advance and then re-heated in the microwave; but are better done at the last moment, having previously prepared the vegetables.

Sweet and Sour Courgettes

Not, in fact, Chinese as it sounds; but based on an old Italian recipe.

This, and the recipe for Red Cabbage (q.v.), have received more compliments than any other vegetables I have ever cooked. So give them a whirl!

INGREDIENTS FOR 6: (ANY LEFTOVERS HEAT UP WELL)

2 lb(900g) Firm Courgettes, headed and tailed

4 tablespoons(4 × 15ml) Good Olive Oil

4 tablespoons(4 × 15ml) White Wine Vinegar

2 tablespoons(2 × 15ml) Caster Sugar

1 teaspoon(5ml) Powdered Cinnamon

Salt and freshly ground Black Pepper.

Equipment: A wide and deep frying pan, or similar.

METHOD:

1. If the courgettes weigh more than 3 oz(90g) each, slice thickly and place them in a colander with a good sprinkling of fine salt. Leave for 1 hour only. The salt will draw out excess moisture from middle-aged vegetables. If left for too long the courgettes will start to go mushy.

If they are small, simply slice and proceed.

2. If you have salted the courgettes dry them on kitchen towel.

3. Fry the courgettes in the olive oil over a medium flame. When they are half cooked (but still firm), sprinkle with the cinnamon and add the sugar and vinegar.

4. Season with plenty of pepper and add salt if your vegetables weren't pre-salted. Mix well.

5. Continue to cook until the courgettes are tender, turning them over in their juices.

* Can be prepared ahead up to this point. They re-heat easily and will in fact improve if kept overnight.

Spinach with Olive Oil

In medieval times, butter was in very short supply, as cows had not yet been reared to supply gallons of milk, as they do now.

Indeed they produced barely enough to feed their calves.

Olive oil was commonly used as a lubricator. It finally fell from grace under the Victorians - only to return with a vengeance now.

This is a 15th. century recipe for cooking spinach: and very good it is too!

INGREDIENTS FOR 4:

2 lb(1 kilo) Fresh Spinach

3 tablespoons(3 × 15ml) Good Olive Oil

A few grates from a whole Nutmeg

A little Salt

EQUIPMENT:

Big stainless steel saucepan, with a close-fitting lid.

METHOD:

1. Wash the spinach carefully and, unless they are baby leaves, strip the leaves away from their tough central core.

2. Transfer the leaves to the saucepan. They will carry enough water from their washing to make more unnecessary.

3. Cover and cook over a medium flame for 5 minutes, stirring once half-way through.

4. Drain the spinach well and press thoroughly to extract excess water.

5. Roughly chop, then return to the pan with the olive oil, salt and grated nutmeg.

6. Gently reheat, coating the leaves with their flavourings.

*Can be prepared an hour ahead and re-heated (a microwave oven is ideal for this). The spinach will lose it's bright colour if left for too long.

Traditional Ratatouille

Along with Gratin Dauphinois (q.v.) this is among the most abused of dishes, sometimes being bastardized by the addition of mushrooms, and suchlike - and more often than not being produced as a watery mass.

However, if you follow the instructions given here, you will have a dish full of delight.

The main secret is the sealing of each vegetable separately - so preserving its individual flavour before the final amalgamation.

EQUIPMENT:

Big ovenproof casserole with a close fitting lid.

INGREDIENTS FOR A GENEROUS 6:

1 big Onion, peeled and roughly chopped

2 big cloves of Garlic, peeled and chopped

4 fl.oz(110ml) Good Olive Oil

1 batch of Warm Tomato Coulis (q.v.) or a 400g tin of Chopped Tomatoes and their juice

1 lb(450g) Firm Aubergines, topped, then thickly sliced and put in a colander, sprinkled with a teaspoon of salt and left for an hour to drain

1 lb(450g) Firm Courgettes, headed and tailed, then thickly sliced. If they are big salt them in a similar way to the aubergines

1 lb(450g) Sweet Peppers, cored and de-seeded, then cut into pieces about 1in.(3cm) square

1 teaspoon(5ml) Herbes de Provence

Freshly ground Black Pepper and a little Salt.

2 oz(60g) stoned Black Olives, a little chopped Flat Parsley or torn fresh Basil (optional garnishes)

METHOD:

1. Gently fry the onions and garlic in a little of the olive oil, until they soften. Transfer to the main casserole, leaving as much oil behind as possible.

2. Dry the aubergine pieces with kitchen towel. Fry them - in batches if necessary until they seal on both sides, adding more oil as it's needed. Transfer to the main casserole, again leaving as much oil behind as possible.

3. Repeat this process, first with the courgettes and then with the peppers - so that each vegetable is individually sealed.

4. Sprinkle with the herbs, and season with a little salt (as you have already added some) and plenty of freshly ground pepper. Add the tomatoes or the coulis and mix well together.

5. Cover, then cook in the pre-heated oven for 40 minutes. Remove the lid - stir and cook for 10 minutes more, or until a sharp knife cuts through a pepper easily.

6. Check the seasonings, bearing in mind that if you are serving the dish cold, flavours weaken. Mix in the black olives, if using.

Serve warm or cold as a starter or vegetable - sprinkled with roughly chopped flat parsley or a few torn basil leaves.

* Greatly improves if prepared a day or more ahead. Re-heat gently.

Fried Radicchio

Not often thought of as a cooked vegetable, Radicchio takes seconds to cook in a deep fryer, if you have the vegetable pieces breadcrumbed in advance.

EQUIPMENT:

A deep fryer or a deep pan and basket and a sugar thermometer

INGREDIENTS FOR 4:

1 big head of Radicchio

2 oz(60g) Flour, sieved

2 × No.3 Eggs, lightly beaten

Salt and freshly ground Pepper

4 oz(115g) Dried Breadcrumbs.

METHOD:

1. Cut the radicchio into quarters, through the root.

2. Put the eggs in a bowl and mix with a little salt and pepper. Put the breadcrumbs onto a plate.

3. Put the flour on a big plate and one at a time shower each radicchio piece with flour, then dip each piece in the beaten egg - then straight into breadcrumbs.

4. Cover completely with the crumbs, then shake off any excess.

* Can be prepared ahead of time up to this point and kept in the fridge.

5. Heat the fryer to 400F, 200C.

6. Deep fry the pieces until the crumbs are golden - about 1 minute.

7. Drain on kitchen paper and serve as a vegetable or as part of a starter with lemon wedges.

Carrot Puree

Try and find nice old carrots for this recipe - don't be tempted to leave out the garlic, as it gives the whole dish a real lift.

EQUIPMENT:

A food processor or Mouli-Legume; a steamer (optional).

INGREDIENTS FOR 6:

2 lb(900g) Old Carrots, peeled, headed and tailed, then sliced into thick rounds

1 big or 2 medium cloves of Garlic, peeled and chopped

2 oz(60g) Butter

2 tablespoons(2 × 15ml) Cream

Salt and freshly ground Pepper.

METHOD:

1. Boil, or better still, steam the carrots and garlic for about 15 minutes - or until very tender.

2. Purée the vegetables in a processor or mouli-legume while they are still warm.

3. Add the butter and cream and season with salt and freshly ground pepper, then mix well.

* Can be prepared ahead up to this point and gently re-heated.

Braised Red Cabbage

A recipe I've developed over the years for this underrated vegetable. Re-heats easily and improves if kept.

INGREDIENTS FOR 6:

1 small Red Cabbage, about 2 lb(1 kilo)

4 oz(115g) Butter

1 medium Onion, peeled and chopped

1 big or 2 medium cloves of Garlic, peeled and chopped

1 big or 2 small Dessert Apples, peeled, cored and coarsely chopped

6 fl.oz(170ml) Heavy Red Wine

3 fl.oz(85ml) Wine Vinegar

1 oz(30g) Sugar

The Zest and the sieved Juice from 1 big or 2 medium Oranges

1 big pinch of Dried Thyme

A few grates of Fresh Nutmeg

The corner of a teaspoon(1mg) Powdered Cinnamon

Salt and freshly ground Pepper.

EQUIPMENT:

A flameproof casserole with a close fitting lid.

METHOD:

1. Take any damaged leaves off the cabbage, then cut it into quarters through the core.

2. Slice away this hard central stalk, the slice the cabbage into slices the thickness of your little finger. Rinse with cold water and drain. Heat the oven to Gas 3, 325F, 160C.

3. Melt the butter in the casserole over a medium flame, then add the cabbage, onions and garlic. Cook for 2 minutes, then add the remaining ingredients, mix well together and bring to the boil.

4. Cover and cook in the oven for 90 minutes.

5. Check the seasoning and try a cabbage stalk. It is good with a little bite remaining. If not quite cooked return to the oven for a few more minutes.

* Can be prepared ahead up to this point and reheated. If keeping for any length of time the cabbage will continue to soften because of the action of the wine and vinegar.

Gratin Dauphinois

This has become one of the most abused dishes of all time, Ratatouille (q.v.) is another that springs to mind . We all have our favourite potato gratins, but please don't call any of them dauphinois unless they are. Most of them bare little resemblance to the dish which one eats in the lower Alps of the Dauphine.

The dish should be perfumed with garlic, plenty, not just a token amount - and please no eggs or cheese toppings!

INGREDIENTS:

2 lbs(1 kilo) waxy rather than floury Potatoes - the big Cyprus or Egyptian potatoes (Nicola's) are ideal

1 pint(600ml) Full fat Milk

8 fl.oz(230ml) Double Cream

4 medium cloves Garlic, peeled and finely chopped

1 teaspoon (5ml) Cornflour

Salt and freshly ground Black Pepper

EQUIPMENT:

A deep (3 ins/70mm will do) oven-proof gratin dish

METHOD:

1. Peel the potatoes and keep covered in cold water. Heat the oven to Gas 3, 325F, 160C.

2. Have a chopping board in front of you, plus your chopped garlic, salt and pepper within reach.

3. Dissolve the cornflour in a little cold water and set aside.

4. Cut the potatoes into fine slices; on no account put them in water at this stage as the starch they hold helps thicken the recipe.

5. Cover the bottom of dish with sliced potato. Sprinkle with salt, pepper and garlic. Continue in this way until until all the potato is used up.

6. Heat the milk until hot, then pour over the potatoes.

7. Give the cornflour another stir, to make sure that it's completely dissolved - mix this with the cream and pour over the potatoes. Mix in a little, but allowing most to stay near the top.

8. Cover the dish loosely with tin foil, making a few holes in the top to allow steam to escape.

9. Put dish in the pre-heated oven, on a baking tray if you're worried about it boiling over.

10. Cook for an hour, then remove the foil covering, increase the oven temperature to Gas 5, 375F, 190C and leave for a further 30 minutes.

11. The top should be golden brown. As potato types vary considerably, test that your gratin is completely cooked, so insert a sharp knife into the middle - it should meet little resistance. If it does, lower the oven temperature a little and cook for a further 15 minutes.

Serve.

* Can be prepared ahead up to this point.

The dish reheats very well, either in the oven or in a microwave. You might find, however, that the potato has absorbed all the liquid - so a little more milk or cream worked in, without spoiling the appearance, might be necessary.

The best ever Chips

There are three simple secrets in the making of first class chips-

1. The type of potatoes used: use Desiree, Maris Pipers or King Edwards. Fish and chip shops use Majestics, for the simple reason that they absorb very little oil and keep their costs down. However hot your oil, you will never make crisp chips with these potatoes.

2. Blanching *correctly.*

3. Use newish oil.

EQUIPMENT:

A deep-fryer with a thermostat or a similar deep pan and a sugar thermometer.

METHOD:

1. Peel and cut the potatoes to the size you prefer. Leave them to soak for an hour in cold water - this will remove excess starch.

2. Drain and dry them carefully with kitchen paper towels.

3. Heat the oil to 350F, 180C and fry the chips until they form a visible skin - about 3 minutes.

* Can be prepared ahead up to this point and when cool can be kept in a fridge overnight, if necessary.

4. When ready to finish, heat the oil to 400F, 200C and fry the chips until golden and crisp.

Drain well and serve sprinkled with a little salt.

When the oil is cool, put it through a fine sieve or coffee filter paper and bottle for use another time.

Pilau Rice

Easy to make and better than anything I've ever had in a restaurant. Reheats easily in a microwave or steamer.

INGREDIENTS FOR 4:

A big pinch of Saffron Threads or a little packet of powder

3 tablespoons(3 × 15ml) Hot Water

6 tablespoons(6 × 15ml) Sunflower or Groundnut Oil

1 Cinnamon Stick

6 Cardamom Pods

4 whole Cloves

3 medium Onions, peeled and sliced

2 big cloves of Garlic, peeled and chopped

2 teaspoons(2 × 5ml) finely chopped Ginger Root

9 oz(250g) Basmati Rice

1 pint(570ml) Beef Stock (q.v.) or half a stock cube dissolved in water

A little freshly ground Pepper.

METHOD:

1. Soak the saffron in the hot water for 15 minutes.
2. Heat the oil in a deep pan over a medium heat, then add the cinnamon, cardamom pods and cloves and fry for a few minutes.
3. Add the onions and fry for about 10 minutes, or until golden - do not allow to burn.
4. Add the garlic, ginger and rice. Mix well, to coat the rice, then fry for 5 minutes - stirring occasionally.
5. Add the stock and bring to the boil.
6. *Simmer*, uncovered, for 10 minutes.
7. Stir in the saffron and it's liquid.
8. Cook for a further 2 minutes, or until the rice has absorbed the liquid.
9. Season with a little pepper and check that there is enough salt - unless you are an addict you should'nt need any, as the stock will be well flavoured.

Mashed Potato

This dish can so often be watery and disappointing; generally because the wrong type of potatoes have been used. As potatoes are fairly bland, you also have to be bold with the seasonings to bring out their true flavour.

EQUIPMENT:

A potato masher or better still a Mouli-legume (available from most cookery shops). On no account be tempted to use a food processor, or you will end up with something resembling glue.

INGREDIENTS FOR 4:

2 lb(1 kilo) Desiree or King Edward Potatoes

5 fl.oz(140ml) Hot Milk

4 oz(110g) Butter or 5 fl.oz(140ml) Good Olive Oil

Freshly grated Nutmeg

Plenty of Salt and freshly ground Pepper.

METHOD:

1. Wash the potatoes, but leave them unpeeled.
2. If you want the best mashed potatoes ever, bake them in the oven, allow to cool slightly and then scoop out their flesh - the skins can be deep fried later as Crisy Potato Skins.
3. If this seems too much trouble, boil - or better still - steam them until they are cooked; allow them to cool a little - then remove their skins.
4. Which ever method you have chosen, mash or pass them through a mouli-legume while they are still warm.
5. Blend in the other ingredients. Checking, when the mixture is smooth, that you have enough salt and pepper.

* Can be prepared ahead up to this stage and gently re-heated (a microwae is ideal for this). If keeping overnight, you may have to mix in a little more milk to stop the mixture being too dry.

Garlic Mashed Potatoes

Add 2 big or 4 medium peeled cloves of garlic to the potatoes when boiling.

Then mash and proceed as above.

This will give you a pleasant garlic taste, without being overpowering.

Mayonnaise

Very easy to make either with a hand whisk - Method One, or in a Food Processor - Method Two. The main thing to remember is the importance of adding the oil very slowly (particularly to start off with) into the egg yolk mixture.

The lemon juice has the reputation of nullifying any bacteria the eggs might hold.

Finished mayonnaise, should however, always be kept at fridge temperature; so if you use any for a barbecue or some such event, do not be tempted to keep any leftovers, however tempting this might be!

INGREDIENTS FOR EITHER METHOD:

3 × No.3 Egg Yolks (freeze the whites for another occasion)

1 teaspoon(5ml) Dijon Mustard

Juice of half a Lemon, sieved

10 fl.oz(300ml) Sunflower Oil - or 7 fl.oz(200ml) Sunflower Oil and 3 fl.oz(100ml) good Olive Oil

A big pinch of fine Salt and a few grinds of freshly ground pepper (black is fine, but will leave a few dark flecks.

METHOD ONE: (BY HAND OR ELECTRIC WHISK)

1. Stand a clean and dry glass or stainless steel bowl on a cloth, to stop it moving around. Add the egg yolks, lemon juice and mustard.
2. Whisk the mixture until a consistent colour, then add the oil a dessertspoon (10ml) at a time - whisking to incorporate fully before adding any more.
3. When you have have used a third of the oil in this way, you can speed up slightly - but always being careful never to add more until your previous additions have been absorbed.
4. When all the oil has been added, season with salt and pepper.

Chill.

METHOD TWO: (FOOD PROCESSOR)

1. In a very clean and dry processor bowl, combine the yolks, lemon juice and mustard and process for 20 seconds.
2. With the machine switched on, add the oil, a dessertspoon full at a time, mixing until the ingredients are well incorporated before adding any further oil.
3. Continue until all the oil has been absorbed: it will be possible to be a little more adventurous with the oil once you have added the first third.
4. When all the oil has been incorporated, season with a little salt and pepper.

Chill.

Mayonnaise made in a food processor tends to be thicker than that made by hand; if this upsets you, it can be thinned down with a little tepid water at any stage

Aioli

Serve as a dip with raw vegetables or with cold fish. The original and traditional form of garlic mayonnaise (the history of which stretches back many centuries and which rather muddlingly gives it's name to a Provencale dish of crudite accompanying the said same sauce).

INGREDIENTS:

    1 batch of Mayonnaise (q.v.)

    4 big cloves of Garlic, peeled.

METHOD:

    1. Chop the garlic finely and blend well with the mayonnaise.

    Chill.

A purist would tell you that the whole sauce should be made with a pestle and mortar. This might be true, but excellent results are obtained using this simple method.

Cheats Rouille

Found more often than not in restaurants these days as an accompaniment for Mediterranean Fish Soup (q.v.). The recipe for true Rouille is given elsewhere in this book and is worth the little extra effort if you have some Fish Soup to use as it's base.

INGREDIENTS:

    1 batch of Aioli (see above)

    1 tablespoon (15ml) of Tomato Puree

    $^1/_2$ teaspoon(2ml) Cayenne Pepper

    A big pinch of powdered Saffron or some strands soaked in very little warm water.

METHOD:

    1. Add all the other ingredients to the Aioli and mix well.

    Chill.

Harissa can be used to replace the tomato puree and cayenne.

Prawn Cocktail Sauce

This once fashionable, and sometimes delicious, starter must be due for a revival. The quality of the dish rests on making an excellent sauce and buying shell-on North Atlantic prawns (which have much more flavour. Here is the easy to make sauce.

INGREDIENTS FOR FOUR:

Half a batch of Mayonnaise (q.v.) or 8 fl.oz(230ml) bought mayonnaise.

6 tablespoons(6 × 15ml) Tomato Ketchup

1 teaspoon(5ml) Worchestershire Sauce

A few drops of Tabasco Sauce

Juice of half a Lemon, sieved.

METHOD:

1. Combine the ingredients and mix well together.

Can be stored in the fridge, in a screw-top jar, for up to a week. If it becomes too thick, it can be diluted with a little tepid water.

Grilled Garlic and Tomato Mayonaise

Very good with cold meat at a picnic, or as a barbecue dip.

INGREDIENTS:

1 batch of Homemade Mayonnaise (q.v.), or the equivalent amount of good bought mayonnaise.

5 cloves of Garlic, peeled

3 big Tomatoes, peeled by quickly dipping into boiling water

1 tablespoon(15ml) Tomato Puree

10 Fresh Basil leaves, torn into small pieces (do not use dried basil, omit altogether if you can't find fresh)

A teaspoon(5ml) Caster Sugar.

METHOD:

1. Cut the skinned tomatoes in half and gently squeeze out as many pips as you can, then grill them with the garlic until they are charred. Remove and allow to cool.

2. Chop the garlic and tomatoes and add them to the mayonnaise with the other ingredients.

3. Refrigerate.

Will keep in the fridge for 2-3 days.

Remoulade Sauce

Delicious with simple fish dishes and cold meats (as a more robust version of Tartare Sauce)

INGREDIENTS FOR A GENEROUS HALF PINT(300ML):

1 batch of Mayonnaise (q.v.) or 12 fl.oz(300ml) good bought mayonnaise

1 hard-boiled Egg, peeled and chopped

2 tablespoons(2 × 15ml) Dijon Mustard

1 tablespoon(15ml) Gherkins, chopped

1 tablespoon(15ml) Capers, roughly chopped

1 tablespoon(15ml) fresh Parsley, chopped

A little fresh Chervil, chopped

A little fresh tarragon, chopped

1 dessertspoon(10ml) Anchovy Essence - if using for fish

Test for Salt and Pepper, especially if using bought mayonnaise.

METHOD:

1. Mix all the ingredients together and check the seasoning.

Must be kept refrigerated: will then last for a few days.

Rouille

Rouille, meaning rust, is a traditional accompaniment for Mediterrranean Fish Soup (q.v.).

Even in France one is often given a mixture resembling Cheats Rouille (q.v.) which although still delicious, in it's own way, does'nt compare with this ambrosial ointment.

While I want to encourage you to make your own soup, more than passable versions are available in glass jars from large supermarkets and specialist shops. I have yet to find anything remotely satisfactory coming from a tin.

EQUIPMENT:

Food Processor.

INGREDIENTS:

2 cloves of Garlic, peeled

1 small tin of Sweet Red Peppers, drained: or 2 Red Peppers, skinned, seeded and roughly chopped

4 ins(10cm) French Bread, with the crusts removed

2 tablespoons(2 × 15ml) good Olive Oil

$\frac{1}{2}$ pint of the finished hot fish soup

$\frac{1}{2}$ teaspoon(3ml) Cayenne Pepper, or more to taste - before adding more remember that its strength will increase over a short period of time.

METHOD:

1. Turn the bread into crumbs, in the food processor; persevere until any trace of a lump has gone - as they will be exaggerated when you add the hot soup.

2. Add the red peppers, garlic and olive oil and process again.

3. Add the cayenne pepper and the hot fish soup. Process until smooth.

Allow to cool.

Keeps for a few days, in a screw-top jar, in the fridge: it's life is restricted to that of the fish soup.

Garlic Butter

Always a good standby to have in the fridge, as it keeps well. Look at the sell-by date on the butter packet to discover the shelf life. The trick is to shape the finished butter like a sausage and then wrap it in foil: in this way you can slice medallions off whenever you like.

Can also be frozen, but remember that garlic tends to go bitter after about a month in the freezer.

EQUIPMENT:

Food Processor. This recipe can also easily be made by hand, but be careful to only soften (and not melt the butter) - otherwise all the solids will go to the bottom of your mixture.

INGREDIENTS:

1 250g packet of Butter - look at the sell by date

4 medium cloves of Garlic, peeled

2 tablespoons(2 × 15ml) chopped Shallots or mild (Spanish) Onions

2 tablespoons(2 × 15ml) chopped Parsley

Freshly ground Black Pepper and a little salt if the butter is slightly or unsalted.

METHOD:

1. Finely chop the garlic, parsley and shallots in the processor.

2. Cut the butter into manageable pieces, then add to the processor bowl and mix well together.

3. Season to taste.

Store as described above.

Anchovy Butter

As an alternative and particularly good with snails, add the following to the above mixture and blend well -

4 Anchovy Fillets, chopped

1 dessertspoon(10ml) Pernod or Ricard

A tablespoon(15ml) of Ground Almonds.

Store as for Garlic Butter.

Pesto Sauce

Although widely available in jars in supermarkets, none will approach the recipe given below. Never be tempted to use dry basil, it simply won't work.

Basil plants are easy to find, but rather fussy about where they live; they like warmth but not wind or draughts. They are still better value than a packet of fresh basil.

Once made, the sauce will keep for up to 2 weeks in the fridge, although it might lose a little colour. Stir well before using, as all the goodies go to the bottom.

EQUIPMENT:

Food Processor

INGREDIENTS:

The leaves from 4 sprigs of fresh Basil

2 big or 4 medium cloves of Garlic, peeled

2 oz(60g) freshly grated Parmesan

1 oz(30g) Pine Nuts

8 fl.oz(230ml) Good Olive Oil

A little Salt and plenty of freshly grated Pepper

METHOD:

1. Combine all the ingredients in a food processor and blend well without over-processing.

Use as a sauce for pasta or to stir into Pesto Soup (q.v.).

Fresh Parmesan Sauce

This sauce goes particularly well with Spinach Mousse (q.v). It is very simple to make, but does need 5 minutes constant attention.

It can, however, be made before your guests arrive, then gently re-heated. Do not refrigerate, as it tends to separate when you try to bring it back to life. If this happens, for any reason, a little extra cream stirred in will bind it.

The black pepper and chopped parsley are important ingredients, as they take away much of the inherent richness.

INGREDIENTS FOR 6:

¹/₂ pint(284ml) of Double Cream; single will not do for this sauce.

2oz(56g) of grated Fresh Parmesan (do not be tempted to use dried).

1 heaped tablespoon of freshly chopped Parsley.

A little Salt plus plenty of freshly ground Black Pepper.

METHOD:

1. Mix the cream and cheese together in a small saucepan over a very low heat.

2. Stir continuously so that the cheese slowly melts without catching on the bottom of the pan.

3. When the cheese has melted add the parsley, salt and pepper.

Pour over the Spinach Mousses.

Warm Tomato Coulis

A good basic tomato sauce for making Ratatouille (q.v.), Aubergine Provencal (q.v.) and serving with mousses such as Warm Gateau of Chicken Livers (q.v.).

INGREDIENTS:

2 tablespoons(2 × 15ml) good Olive Oil

2 oz(60g) chopped Onions

2 cloves of Garlic, chopped

1 400g tin of Chopped Tomatoes

2 teaspoons(2 × 5ml) Tomato Puree

2 sprigs of Parsley, chopped

Salt and freshly ground black pepper, to taste.

METHOD:

1. Heat the oil, in a stainless steel saucepan, over a low heat.

2. Add the chopped onion and garlic, then *sweat* until the onion looks translucent - about 3 minutes.

3. Add the tomatoes, puree and chopped parsley. Mix well together.

4. Maintaining the low heat, cook for 30 minutes.

5. Season with salt and pepper.

6. Sieve, if using as a sauce for mousses; otherwise this is not necessary.

* Can be prepared ahead up to this point; but be careful when reheating, as it can spit and make a terrible mess!

Caramelized Tomato Sauce

Quick and easy to make, and more delicious than you could imagine such a simple recipe could be. An excellent accompaniment to simply cooked fish. See Frying Fish Fillets (q.v.).

INGREDIENTS:

1 lb(450g) Fresh Tomatoes, or if lacking flavour a 400g tin of the best whole tomatoes

1 big clove of Garlic, peeled and chopped

8 fl.oz(230ml) good Olive Oil

Salt and freshly ground Pepper

1 oz(30g) Butter.

METHOD:

1. Cut the tomatoes in two and de-seed and juice as well as possible. Pre-heat oven to Gas 6, 400F, 200C.

2. Pour the olive oil into roasting tin, spread the tomatoes out on top and roast in the oven for 30 minutes. The tomatoes should look slightly burnt, don't worry, this is fine.

3. Place the roasting tin on a medium gas ring, then add the chopped garlic and 1 pint(560ml) water.

4. *Deglaze* the pan to loosen the tomatoes and cook for a further 30 minutes.

5. Liquidize the sauce, then sieve into a stainless steel saucepan.

6. Season with a little salt and pepper.

* Can be prepared ahead up to this point.

7. Whisk in the butter just before serving.

Spring Onion and White Wine Sauce

Excellent with simply grilled chicken, or as a sauce for mousses such as Gateau of Chicken Livers (q.v.). Can be prepared well ahead and re-heated.

INGREDIENTS FOR 1/2 PINT (PLENTY FOR SIX):

1 bunch of Spring Onions; (trimmed of their root, but with most of the green left on) washed and cut into short lengths.

2 oz(60g) Butter

1 tablespoon(15ml) Flour

7 fl.oz(190ml) Full Fat Milk

3 fl.oz(90ml) Dry White Wine

2 teaspoons(2 × 5ml) Dijon Mustard

7 fl.oz(190ml) Single Cream

Salt and freshly ground pepper

Juice of ½ lemon, sieved.

METHOD:

1. Chop the spring onions finely by hand, or roughly in a food processor.

2. Melt the butter in a stainless steel saucepan, then *sweat* the onions for 3-4 minutes.

3. Add the flour and the mustard and mix well in.

4. Gradually add the milk, stirring continuously to incorporate. Cook over a low heat, until thick and smooth.

5. Add the wine and cook for a further 2 minutes.

6. Add the cream and lemon juice, then season with salt and pepper.

7. *Simmer* for a further 3 minutes; then remove from the heat, as overcooking will lose the fresh colour.

Serve.

Keeps well for a few days, in the fridge, as long as you use fresh milk and cream.

Fish Stock

This stock is very quick and easy to make. In fact it should'nt be cooked for longer than 30 minutes, as tends to become bitter.

Your local fishmonger will be only too pleased to keep you some bones (called frames by fishermen), especially if you buy some fish as well!

Sole bones are the best, followed by other flat fish: avoid anything oily - such as salmon, herring or mackerel.

INGREDIENTS FOR 2 PINTS:

3 lbs(1.5 kilos) of fish heads and bones, thoroughly washed

10 fl.oz(300ml) Dry White Wine

1 big Onion, peeled and chopped

2 oz(60g) Carrot, peeled and chopped

2 oz(60g) Leek, peeled and chopped

1 stick of Celery, or a few leaves from the top of the head

1 Bay Leaf

2 Sprigs of Parsley

1 Clove

2 pints(1 litre) cold water.

METHOD:

1. Put the washed bones in a big saucepan.

2. Add the other ingredients and bring to the boil, skimming off any froth.

3. *Simmer* for 30 minutes, skimming if necessary.

4. Strain through a fine sieve.

When cold it should be refrigerated, where it will keep for a few days, or longer if boiled up each day.

Or freeze in carefully labelled small units (such as ice cube trays or old cream containers). Once frozen the stock cubes can be kept in a plastic freezer container and used as required.

Hot Emulsion Sauces

These should hold no fears for you. If you follow the directions nothing can go wrong; you can also make them just before your guests arrive, so your confidence will have the added boost that you could have another attempt if need be.

Plan ahead: If making Hollandaise or Bearnaise sauces find yourself a double saucepan or a heatproof bowl that fits securely into one of your saucepans and will serve as a bain-marie. Have the required amount of butter cut into pieces and at room temperature - if it is too cold it can jam in the blades of an electric whisk and fly across the room in an alarming way! If using a hand-held electric mixer make sure that the flex reaches the cooker hob. Plug it in and have it ready, so there is no last minute panic. A small manual ballon whisk will serve just as well.

Hollandaise Sauce

Serve with fish, chicken and vegetables.

INGREDIENTS FOR 6:

6oz(170g) Unsalted Butter; at room temperature and cut into walnut-sized pieces.

1 tablespoon cold water.

3 Egg Yolks (freeze the whites for another occasion)

1 tablespoon Lemon Juice, sieved (about $^1/_2$ a lemon)

A little Salt + freshly ground Pepper (white if you want to avoid black specks)

METHOD:

1. Put water in the lower half of the bain-marie, making sure that when the top half is added it will not touch the water. Bring to the boil, then lower the heat to maintain a bare *simmer*.

2. Put the water, lemon juice and egg yolks into the top half of your bain marie and lightly whisk.

3. Place the bowl, with the egg mixture, over the simmering water.

4. Start whisking with one hand, while slowly adding butter with the other. Only add more butter as the preceeding piece has melted and been incorporated.

5. The mixture will start to thicken as it rises above blood temperature.

6. When all the butter has been used and the sauce is thick enough to coat the back of a spoon, remove from the heat.

7. Season to taste.

* The sauce can be held at this stage for about 90 minutes, in a cool part of the kitchen, maintaining a certain amount of heat over the hot water.

A slightly inferior, but more stable sauce, can be made by adding half a teaspoon of cornflour or arrowroot to the cold water, before cooking - making sure that it is completely dissolved.

Bearnaise Sauce

Serve with beef, chicken or as a livelier version of Hollandaise.

Made in much the same way as Hollandaise, but using a reduction instead of lemon juice as it's base. This reduction can be prepared well ahead of time. Indeed once made made can be strained and kept for days in a larder or fridge. The smell of reducing vinegar needs to be well clear before your guests arrive.

INGREDIENTS FOR 6:

For the reduction -

4 fl.oz(100ml) white wine or cider vinegar.

2 teaspoons(2 × 5ml spoons) of chopped fresh tarragon or 1 teaspoon of dried tarragon.

2 teaspoons of chopped shallots or mild onions.

A small piece of bay leaf.

A few whole peppercorns (optional)

For the sauce -

3 egg yolks (freeze the whites for another occasion)

6oz(170g) Unsalted Butter

Salt and freshly ground pepper (white if you want to avoid black specks).

METHOD:

1. Combine the reduction ingredients in a stainless steel or glass saucepan (aluminium is best avoided as the vinegar will attack it).

2. Put over a medium heat, then *reduce* to one quarter of its volume.

3. Strain through a sieve into a clean bowl, pushing down well to extract as much flavour as possible. Throw the solids away.

*This is your sauce base and can be prepared the day before.

4. To make - follow instructions for Hollandaise Sauce, using all the reduction mixed into your egg yolks.

Variations on Hollandaise Sauce.

Anchovy Sauce

Delicious with grilled fish and Spinach Mousse (q.v,)

INGREDIENTS FOR 6:

1 batch of Hollandaise Sauce (q.v.)

4 tinned Anchovy Fillets.

2 tablespoons of warm water.

METHOD:

1. Make the Hollandaise Sauce as diected.

2. Make a purée of the anchovy fillets, mix them with 2 tablespoons of warm water.

3. Mix the puree with the Hollandaise.

Serve. Difficult to reheat, as the sauce will split. But can be prepared ahead of time - see Hollandaise Sauce.

Mustard Sauce

Delicious with white fish and ham.

INGREDIENTS FOR 6:

1 batch of Hollandaise Sauce (q.v.)
2 teaspoons of made-up English Mustard
2 teaspoons of Dijon Mustard.

METHOD:

1. Mix all the ingredients together.

Serve warm or cold. See under Hollandaise Sauce about making ahead of time.

Orange Bakewell Tart (for 4-6)

A pudding that can be made a few hours before your guests arrive, and left at room temperature; or better still prepared earlier up to stage 6, refrigerated, then put in the oven as you serve the main course. Delicious with whipped cream, or for a real treat a scoop of Praline and Tia Maria Parfait (q.v). Using ground almonds instead of rice is an unnecessary extravagance, but be careful to be light with the almond essence and not to economise by using almond flavouring instead.

EQUIPMENT NEEDED:

1 × 8in flan tin. Food processor if using Quick Pâté Sucree.

INGREDIENTS;

Half a batch Pate Sucree (q.v) at room temperature - the remainder makes delicous biscuits, can be frozen for another time or you could make 2 tarts, as they reheat successfully.

Half a jar of marmalade, gently heated then sieved; the peel thrown away.

4 oz(125g) unsalted butter

4 oz(125g) caster sugar

1 × No.2 egg,lightly beaten

4 oz(125g) ground rice

Half a teaspoon almond essence.

METHOD:

1. Pre-heat the oven to gas mark 5,375F,190C.

2. Lightly butter the flan tin, roll out the pastry quite thinly on a lightly floured board, and use it to line the flan tin, being careful to push it right into the corners; any holes can be repaired with loose pastry. Refrigerate while you prepare the filling.

3. Melt the butter over a gentle heat, and stir in the caster sugar until dissolved, remove from the heat and cool slightly.

4. Gently heat the sieved marmalade, then spread evenly over the pastry base.

5. Add the beaten egg, ground rice and almond essence to the butter mixture. Mix well and spread the mixture evenly over the marmalade.

* Can be prepared ahead up to this point and kept overnight in the fridge.

6. Bake for 35 minutes, or until risen & golden. Rest for 5 minutes before removing from the tin.

Left over slices can be gently reheated in a microwave.

Bananas in Foil

Both simple to prepare and delicious to eat. Based on a recipe of Michel Guerard's - the inventor of Cuisine Minceur. This simplified version will become a favourite.

INGREDIENTS FOR 4:

8 ripe bananas, peeled

1 × 400g. tin of Apricots, in natural juice rather than sugar syrup

2 Vanilla Pods

2 tablespoons(2 × 15ml) Caster Sugar

4 tablespoons(4 × 15ml) Water.

EQUIPMENT:

Food Processor; 4 pieces of tin foil 12ins(30cm) square.

METHOD:

1. Drain and liquidize the apricots.

2. Pre-heat the oven to Gas 7, 425F, 220C.

3. Melt the sugar in the water over a low heat; when it has dissolved, bring to the boil and remove from the heat.

4. Split the vanilla pods lengthways.

5. Assemble by placing the 2 bananas in the centre of each square of foil with half a vanilla pod between them. Share the liquidized apricots between them.

6. Fold the foil to make individual parcels and seal carefully.

* Can be prepared ahead up to this point and kept in the fridge.

7. Bake on a tray in the oven for 20 minutes.

Allow your guests to unwrap their own parcels. The vanilla pods can be washed and re-used.

Thin Apple Tart

Very quick to make, as long as you have your tart assembled and the oven heated before your meal.

FOR EACH PERSON:

2 dessert Apples, peeled, halved and cored

1 thin 5 in(12.5cm) round of Puff Pastry, pricked all over with a fork to decrease rising

1 teaspoon(5ml) Caster Sugar

A knob (about 15g) Unsalted Butter

A little icing sugar and a blow-lamp to finish (optional)

Caramel Sauce (q.v.) to accompany.

METHOD:

1. Cut the apples into very thin slices and arrange around the pastry base, starting at the edge and working in: leave a small gap around the perimeter edge so the pastry can rise a little. This will also help you see when the pastry is cooked.

2. Sprinkle the apples with sugar, then dot with butter.

* Can be prepared ahead up to this point and kept in the fridge for up to 2 hours (although the apples will discolour slightly, when the tart has cooked this will not be noticeable).

3. Have the oven ready at Gas 6, 400F, 200C.

4. Bake on a lightly floured baking sheet for 10 minutes, or until the pastry is golden brown around the edges.

5. If being very smart, sprinkle with a little icing sugar and brown with a blow lamp (if using a gas lamp, have it properly warmed, or it will keep going out annoyingly each time you tilt it).

Serve surrounded with a little Caramel Sauce (q.v.).

Steamed Chocolate Pudding

Far removed from a school pudding, this pudding can be cooked in advance and reheated in the steamer, but is lighter if cooked freshly. A few minutes longer in the steamer while your guests finish their main courses, will do no harm at all. Serve with Chocolate Sauce (q.v.).

EQUIPMENT:

6 dariole moulds, ramekins or small tea cups; a steamer big enough to hold the above: or one pudding basin.

Tin foil to cover the puddings.

INGREDIENTS FOR 6:

4 oz(115g) Unsalted Butter

4 oz(115g) Caster Sugar

3 × No.3 Eggs, lightly beaten

1 oz(30g) Ground Almonds

4 oz(115g) Self-Raising Flour, sieved

2 oz(60g) Cocoa Powder, sieved

2 fl.oz(60ml) Sweet or medium Sherry

A little butter to wipe over the moulds.

METHOD:

1. Smear a little butter around your chosen moulds and set aside.

2. Cream the butter and sugar with a wooden spoon, until smooth.

3. Mix in the ground almonds, followed by the flour, cocoa sherry and eggs. Gently stir until the mixture is smooth.

4. Share the mixture between the basins - or use just one if you prefer.

5. Cover the containers with buttered foil and losely fix down around the edges.

6. Steam for about 90 minutes (for individual puddings) or 2 hours for one big one; being careful that the steamer-water does'nt dry up.

Turn out and serve, covered in Chocolate Sauce.

Chocolate Mousse

The best Chocolate Mousse ever!

If you know a better one please tell me.

Not the easiest to make, but just needs proper concentration. Keeps well, in the fridge, for a few days.

EQUIPMENT:

Plastic, lidded, freezer container or, if entertaining soon, an attractive bowl in which to present your mousse at the table.

A double saucepan to form a *bain-marie*

A big bowl, that you can sit on a saucepan of boiling water securely - to form another *bain-marie.*

Hand whisk or hand held electric mixer with a long enough flex to reach your cooker.

INGREDIENTS FOR 8 GLUTTONS:

13 oz(390g) Plain Chocolate; use Bournville or one with a higher cocoa solid content

2 × No.3 Eggs

2 × No.3 Egg Yolks (freeze the whites for another time)

1 pint(560ml) Double Cream

2 fl.oz(60ml) Cognac or Armagnac (something simply labelled brandy will not do)

1 fl.oz(30ml) Tia Maria

METHOD:

1. Melt the chocolate, over warm water, in the small *bain-marie.*

2. While you are doing this, whisk the whole eggs and yolks in the bowl balanced over a saucepan of simmering water. Achieve as hot a sabayon as you dare, without making scrambled eggs! Certainly well over blood heat and fairly thick. Remove from the heat.

3. Add the melted chocolate to the egg mixture and whisk, on a low speed, until well mixed.

4. In a separate bowl, whip the cream with the liquors until bulky, but not over stiff.

5. Add the cream to the chocolate and egg mix and lightly fold-in with a spatula until well combined.

6. Pour into your chosen storage container and refrigerate.

Don't worry that the mixture seems runny, as it will solidify in about 4 hours.

Very good with Coffee Sauce (q.v.).

Warm Chocolate Tarts

These impressive individual tarts can be prepared ahead, so they only take 10 minutes to finish. They can be baked ahead and re-heated, but they will not be so light.
Delicious with Raspberry or Blackberry Coulis (q.v.) and a little cream or Creme Fraiche.

EQUIPMENT:
  4 individual tart tins, loose bottomed if possible

INGREDIENTS FOR 4:
  ¹/₂ batch of Pate Sucree, with the zest from an orange added
  3 × No.3 Egg Yolks (freeze 2 of the whites for another time)
  1 oz(30g) Caster Sugar
  4 oz(115g) Unsalted Butter
  5 oz(160g) Good Dark Chocolate - use the one with the highest cocoa solids: Bournville is satisfactory, some supermarket brands cheaper and better
  1 Egg White
  A pinch of Salt
  A sprinkling of icing sugar to decorate (optional).

METHOD:
  1. Pre-heat the oven to Gas 4, 350F, 180C.
  2. Line the tart tins with the pastry, pierce the base all over with a fork, then bake *blind* for 5 minutes, carefully remove the foil and filling and cook uncovered for a further 5 minutes.
  3. Leave to cool.
  4. For the chocolate filling - break the chocolate into pieces and melt with the butter in a *bain marie*. Remove from the heat and cool slightly.
  5. While the chocolate is melting, whisk the egg yolks and caster sugar with 2 tablespoons (2 × 15ml) of water, in a big bowl, until pale and fluffy.
  6. Combine the chocolate and egg yolk mixtures and mix well.

* Can be prepared a few hours ahead up to this point. If doing so, leave the chocolate mixture at room temperature, so the mixture does'nt solidify. You will need your oven on the same temperature as above.

  7. Whisk the egg white with a pinch of salt, until stiff.
  8. Fold into the chocolate mixture.
  9. Bake for 6 minutes until lightly set.

To serve - unmould, place on a big plate dust with icing sugar and pour coulis on one side and double cream or creme fraiche on the other.

Ice Creams and Frozen Desserts

The flavour of these ice creams will beat anything you can buy. None of the recipes needs any special equipment (and only the more basic ice creams special attention once in the deep freeze), but the alcohol listed in many is a necessary ingredient and stops the finished texture becoming too firm and unmanageable. Supermarket delicatessen departments are a good source of plastic containers suitable for freezing, or you can buy excellent freezer boxes with good close-fitting lids.

It cannot be stressed too strongly that all containers, bowls and utensils must be thoroughly clean; in fact sterilizing items by boiling for a few minutes in water is advisable and will give you complete peace of mind. Once made, cover with a double layer of cling film or a well fitting lid, to stop ice crystals forming. These frozen desserts will keep for a month in a *** deep freeze, but will be at their best for the first week.

Vanilla Ice Cream

This is a very rich ice cream, for a special occasion; for a more everyday version substitute full fat milk for cream.

While a vanilla pod, as opposed to essence, may seem an extravagance, it can be carefully rinsed and used again; or rinsed and dried then placed in a jar of caster sugar to produce vanilla sugar.

INGREDIENTS:

8 egg yolks

3oz(100g) caster sugar

1 pint single cream

1 vanilla pod

METHOD:

1. Put your deep freeze on to fast freeze if possible. Beat the egg yolks and sugar until they are creamy and all the sugar has dissolved.

2. Slowly bring the cream to the boil, with the vanilla pod.

3. Remove the pod and pour the cream on to the eggs and sugar, whisking well all he time.

4. Arrange this bowl over a saucepan of boiling water and, stirring all the time, thicken the mixture until it coats the back of a wooden spoon.

5. Leave the custard to cool completely, then transfer the mixture into your chosen freezing container, sieving if you spot any unsightly lumps of cooked egg.

6. Freeze, stirring or whizzing in a spotlessly clean food processor every half an hour, until nearly frozen. This will ensure a creamy texture.

Brown Bread Ice Cream

Easier than plain vanilla to set smoothly without an ice cream machine, because of the added alcohol, and forever popular with children of all ages.

INGREDIENTS:

1 batch of Vanilla Ice Cream prepared up to the point of freezing.

2 tablespoons of Amontillado (medium) Sherry

3 oz(100g) of fresh wholemeal breadcrumbs (easily made by whizzing bread in a food processor: the crusts are better removed, as they can be stubborn)

2 oz (50g) unsalted butter

3 oz (75g) caster sugar

METHOD:

1. Put your deep-freeze on fast freeze if possible. Add the sherry to the vanilla ice cream, prepared for freezing, as above. Place in the deep freeze, stirring every half hour for 2 hours.

2. Fry the breadcrumbs in the butter until crisp.

3. Add the sugar and let this caramelise, without disturbing more than necessary. Cool completely.

4. Put in a plastic bag, then crush with a rolling pin

5. Add to the ice cream mixture as it is beginning to set. Continue stirring at 30 minute intervals until frozen.

Maple Ice Cream

INGREDIENTS:

$^1/_2$ pint(284ml) Maple Syrup; don't be tempted to use anything but the best, look carefully at the ingredients - maple flavouring will not do!

4 × No.3 Eggs, separated.

$^3/_4$ pint(454ml) Double Cream, whipped until thick and forming soft peaks.

METHOD:

1. Switch your deepfreeze to fast-freeze. Make sure that your freezing container and cooking utensils are scrupulously clean.

2. Put the egg yolks in a heat-proof bowl that will form a *bain marie* with one of your saucepans. Half fill this saucepan with water, making sure that the bottom of the bowl is well clear of the water. Put the saucepan of water, without the bowl, over a medium heat.

3. Boil the maple syrup, then pour over the egg yolks, stirring to mix well.

4. Set the bowl over your saucepan of hot water; beat continually until the mixture thickens.

5. Remove from the heat and allow to cool.

6. Fold the custard into the whipped cream.

7. Whisk the egg whites until very stiff, then gently fold into the cream.

8. Transfer the mixture to your chosen freezing container. Freeze.

9. Remove from freezer every 30 minutes or so, whizz-up in the food processor; then return to your deep freeze. Repeat this 3 times.

Delicious with Tuilles (q.v)

Prune and Armagnac Ice Cream

Delicious! If you're not a believer will change your attitude to prunes.

INGEDIENTS:

8 × No.3 Egg Yolks (freeze the whites for future use)

6oz(170g) Caster Sugar

1lb(454g) Natural Prunes; pre-soaked/ready to eat prunes are not a satisfactory alternative.

2fl.oz(60ml) Armagnac or Cognac: a bottled labelled brandy (even if mentioning Napoleon) will not produce the same result.

1 pint(600ml) Double Cream.

METHOD:

1. Cook the prunes as directed on the packet, or if they are loose - cover with plenty of tea or water, bring to the boil then "simmer" until they are tender (possibly as long as 2 hours.

2. Drain and discard the liquid.

3. Stone the prunes when they are cool enough to handle.

4. Finely chop the prunes by hand: do not be tempted to use a liquidizer, as this will over process them and spoil the texture of the dessert.

5. Put the egg yolks into a big bowl, gradually add the caster sugar while beating, until the mixture forms ribbons.

6. Stir in the roughly chopped prunes and add the Armagnac.

7. In a separate bowl, beat the cream until it holds peaks.

8. Fold the cream into the prune mixture.

Freeze.

The alcohol will ensure that the mixture sets to a manageable consistency. To serve use an ice cream scoop dipped in hot water.

Praline and Tia Maria Parfait

A totally delicious rich ice cream, that needs no attention at all while freezing (because of the sugar and added alcohol). Good simply on its own, or for a special occasion with a Tuille (q.v) or with warm Orange Bakewell Tart (q.v).

INGREDIENTS FOR 8:

6 oz(150 g) shelled almonds - the ones with natural brown skins are best, but white blanched are satisfactory.

6 oz(150g) caster sugar

1 pint (550ml) double cream

4 egg whites (if you've been saving them in the deep freeze use 4 fl oz(120cl)

1 large sherry glass (about 5 fl oz/150ml) of Tia Maria.

EQUIPMENT:

Food processor (or plenty of elbow grease).

METHOD:

1. Set your deep freeze to fast freeze if possible. Make the praline mixture, by combining the nuts and sugar in a heavy saucepan and heating gently until the sugar melts. Resist stirring until the sugar starts to caramelise; once this begins be careful of any spitting sugar.

2. When sugar has completely melted, mix well to coat the nuts.

3. Pour on to an oiled tray (a litle sunflower or vegetable oil, not strong tasting olive) and allow to cool and set. Do not be tempted to refrigerate to speed up the process, as this will make the praline soft.

4. When cold and toffee-like, break into manageable pieces and food process until the mixture resembles sawdust. THIS WILL MAKE AN ALARMING NOISE. If you don't have food processor, put your roughly broken pieces into a strong plastic bag and attack them with a rolling pin: a combination of hammering and rolling with produce the same result.

* The praline powder will keep for a few days at this stage, if held at larder temperature.

5. Whip the cream with the Tia Maria until it is bulky and fairly stiff.

6. Whisk the egg whites until very stiff.

7. Add the praline to the cream mixture and mix thoroughly.

8. Fold, rather than mix, in the whipped egg whites; trying not to knock too much air out of them - but still encorporating fully, so that not too many white flecks are visible.

9. Pour into a very clean container, cover and freeze.

Tuiles and Ice Cream Baskets

Easy to make and a good way of using left over egg whites, that I hope you've been saving in the deep freeze. Tuiles (from the French tiles) will turn any simple pud into something for a special occasion; and by moulding it into a basket, while still warm, you have a homemade container for ice cream. Both tuiles and baskets keep for a few days in an air-tight tin.

INGREDIENTS:

4 oz(115g) Unsalted Butter, softened

7 oz(200g) Plain Flour

8 oz(230g) Caster Sugar

7 Egg Whites (if using from the freezer, 7 fl.oz/190ml)

1 oz(30g) Sesame Seeds

A big pinch of Powdered Ginger

METHOD:

1. Cream the butter, then add the flour, ginger, sesame seeds and egg whites: mix together thoroughly until smooth.

2. Spread out in teaspoons on to a greased baking tray and bake at Gas 5, 375F, 190C, until golden: about 5 - 6 minutes.

3. For tuilles put the individual tiles straight from the oven on to a rolling pin or bottle - they will set into shape almost instantly.

4. For baskets, mould the tile around the outside of a small tea-cup.

If they start setting before you are ready, simply return to the oven for a few seconds to soften them.

Butterscotch Sauce

For Vanilla Ice Cream (q.v)

INGREDIENTS:

8 oz(225g) light muscovado sugar

4 fl oz(120ml) single cream

1 oz(25g) unsalted butter

2 tablespoons of golden syrup

METHOD:

1. Gently heat all the ingredients, stirring occasionally, until the sugar has melted.

2. Bring to the boil, stirring continuously.

3. Cool and serve.

If the sauce becomes too thick in the fridge, carefully mix in a little extra cream.

Chocolate Sauce

Very good warm with Steamed Chocolate Pudding (q.v)

Most recipes list cocoa for making this, without realising that chocolate lovers want the real thing in it's concentrated form. Find plain chocolate with the highest listed cocoa solids content (this will be listed clearly on the label). I've recommended Bournville (at 34%) as a kicking off point. This, or anything higher, possibly supermarket own brands, will be fine. Don't use milk chocolate, just because you prefer it, the cream dilution will leave you with no flavour. The coffee will be unnoticeable, but simply accentuate the flavour of the chocolate.

INGREDIENTS:

A 200g bar of Bournville or similar (see above)

1 teaspoon of instant coffee

10 fl oz(400ml) single cream (maximum)

METHOD:

1. Break the chocolate into chunks into a saucepan and add half the cream and the coffee.

2. Heat gently until the cocolate melts, stirring occasionally. It is important that this is not hurried as too fierce a heat will make the chocolate bitter.

3. Dilute with extra cream until you have the required consistency.

Serve hot, or leave at room temperature if required cold. This sauce can be refrigerated, but will solidify, so extreme care and constant stirring is needed when reheating.

For CHOCOLATE ORANGE SAUCE, add 2 tablespoons of Grand Marnier when melting chocolate. Cointreau will not produce the same result.

Coffee Sauce

Served cold, this is very good with Chocolate Mousse (q.v).

INGREDIENTS:
   6 egg yolks (freeze the whites for future use; e.g. meringues)
   3 tablespoons of caster sugar
   $1/4$ pint(150ml) of strong coffee; good instant will be fine - warm to hot, but not boiling.
   2 tablespoons Tia Maria or Cognac (optional)
   $1/4$ pint(150ml) single cream

METHOD:
   1. Whisk the egg yolks, sugar and coffee in a bowl over hot water until it becomes quite thick.
   2. Mix in the cream and your chosen liqueur.
   3. Cool, the chill.

Caramel Sauce

Very good with Thin Apple Tarts (q,v.).

INGREDIENTS FOR 6 -8:
   5 fl.oz(150g) Water
   9 oz(250g) Caster Sugar
   9 fl.oz(250ml) Double Cream

METHOD:
   1. Mix the sugar and water in a small, heavy-based saucepan.
   2. Melt the sugar over a low heat; then increase the flame and boil until the mixture becomes golden brown. Do not burn, or your sauce will be bitter.
   3. While the sugar is caramelizing, bring the cream to the boil in a larger stainless steel pan, being careful as it will suddenly try to boil over: set aside on the draining board.
   4. Add the caramel to the cream (never the other way round) over the sink, mixing constantly.
   5. Transfer to a low heat and continue stirring until you have a smooth sauce.
   * Can be prepared ahead up to this point. Will keep in the fridge up to the sell-by date of the cream.

Pate Sucree

Very quick and foolproof to make and far superior to anything you can buy. Both the Traditional and the Quick food processor methods produce enough for 2 × 8in (20cm) flan tins or 10 × 4in (10cm) tartlet tins. Any leftover pastry can be stored, in a plastic bag, in the fridge for 2 days or frozen for a future occasion.

For a treat mix in a drop of vanilla essence and some grated orange rind and you can bake some delicious biscuits.

TRADITIONAL METHOD:

INGREDIENTS:

- 7 oz(200g) plain flour
- 2 oz(80g) caster sugar
- 3 egg yolks (the whites can be frozen and used later for meringues; an old cream pot is ideal for this)
- 3oz(100g) unsalted butter, at room temperature, cut into small pieces

METHOD:

1. Sieve the flour on to a work surface or, better still, a big bowl to cut down on the mess. Make a well in the centre.
2. Put the salt, sugar and egg yolks into the well and mix well with your fingertips.
3. Add the butter pieces and gradually work into the flour to form a dough. Knead until well mixed, then form into a ball.
4. Put into a plastic bag, and refrigerate for at least 30 minutes before using.

QUICK PATE SUCREE:

EQUIPMENT:

Food processor.

INGREDIENTS:

- 100 oz(275g) plain flour
- 7 oz(200g) unsalted butter, straight from the fridge
- 1 oz(25g) caster sugar
- 1 egg
- A little ice-cold water

METHOD:

1. Cut the butter into cubes, being careful to keep it cold
2. Combine the flour, sugar and butter in the processor bowl. Process until the mixture resembles coarse breadcrumbs.
3. Add the egg and process for just long enough to mix the ingredients.
4. With the motor running add just enough ice cold water for the dough to form a ball around the blade. Do not overprocess.
5. Dust the pastry with flour and put into a plastic bag. Refrigerate for 30 minutes before using.

Garlic and Sherry Pastry

This pastry lifts cooked flour paste away from being a mere container: it will earn you compliments whenever it is produced. Transforms Leek and Bacon, or Trout and Spring Tarts (q.v.) into gourmet dishes. While the recipe is infallible, very cold butter and the minimum of processing produce the lightest pastry.

EQUIPMENT:

Food Processor.

INGREDIENTS FOR 8 INDIVIDUAL TARTS:

1 big or 2 small cloves of Garlic, peeled

6 oz(170g) Plain White Flour

2.5 oz(70g) very cold Butter, chopped into walnut-sized pieces

Salt and freshly ground pepper

Juice of ¹/₂ Lemon, sieved

1 × No.3 Egg

A little Dry Sherry (about a small sherry glass).

METHOD:

1. Finely chop the garlic in the food processor.
2. Add the flour, plus a little salt and pepper and briefly mix.
3. Add the chopped butter and process for a few seconds, until the mixture resembles breadcrumbs.
4. Add the egg and the lemon juice and process for a further 10 seconds.
5. Now this is where you have to be careful - with the open sherry bottle in one hand, switch on the processor and slowly dizzle in some sherry. Stop as soon as the Pastry forms a ball around the blade.

* Can be prepared ahead up to this stage and stored overnight in the fridge. If you are planning ahead in this way, shape the dough into a large sausage roll, you can then cut medallions from it to form individual tarts. Alternatively, fill your tart tins and finish baking them as required, straight from the fridge.

Unlike most pastry, this dough can be rolled out straight away, but should then be rested in the fridge for at least ¹/₂ hour before baking.

Crisps from Root Vegetables

Excellent with pre-dinner drinks or as game chips with simply roasted poultry or game.
Any root vegetables will do, apart from the obvious potatoes - celeriac, carrots, parsnips for example plus my own favourite beetroot.

EQUIPMENT:

Deep-fryer

METHOD:

1. Peel your chosen vegetables and slice into very thin rounds. Heat clean oil in the deep fryer to 385F, 190C.
2. Soak in cold water for 20 minutes to diminish the starch level.
3. Drain and dry thoroughly in paper towels.
4. Fry the chips for about 3 minutes or until crisp.
5. Drain on more kitchen towels and serve.

These are better freshly cooked, but will keep for a few days in an airtight tin.

Potato Skins

These make a good snack and are popular with kids of all ages. They are particularly good with cream, soured with lemon juice, mixed with chopped fresh chives.

EQUIPMENT:

Deep-fryer

INGREDIENTS:

Potato peelings, kept in cold water. If planning this, peel you potatoes a little thicker than usual.

METHOD:

1. Cover the peelings in cold water, in a saucepan.
2. Bring to the boil, then drain.
*Can be prepared ahead up to this point.
3. Heat clean oil in the deep-fryer to 385F, 190C.
4. Fry for about 3 minutes until golden and crisp.
Drain on kitchen towls and serve.

Lemon or Lime Pickle

A good strong pickle for cold meats, curries and as an accompaniment for a Tagine (q.v.) instead of traditional Preserved Lemons.

A certain amount of foresight is needed, as the pickle needs to be prepared at least a week in advance; and will continue to improve for many months.

EQUIPMENT:

1 litre Preserving Jar or 2 smaller jars (which may fit into a fridge better - see below). A big stainless steel pan.

INGREDIENTS TO FILL A 1 LITRE PRESERVING JAR:

10 Limes or 8 small Lemons, cut into quarters lengthways

2 oz(60g) Fine Sea Salt

1 big or 2 medium Onions, peeled and chopped

8 fl.oz(230ml) White Wine or Cider Vinegar

2 Fresh Red Chillis, de-seeded and finely chopped

1 oz(30g) finely chopped Fresh Ginger

10 whole Cardamom pods

20 whole Allspice berries

12 oz(340g) Caster Sugar.

METHOD:

1. Put the fruit quarters in a glass or stainless steel bowl and sprinkle with the salt. Stand for 6 hours, mixing occasionally.

2. Heat the oven to Gas 2, 300F, 150C. Wash the preserving jar and sterilize by putting in the oven -resting on a tea-towel - for 30 minutes. Be careful that the towel is safe from any flames!

3. Thoroughly wash all the salt from the fruit and throw the liquid they have produced away.

4. Combine all the ingredients with the fruit, in a big stainless steel saucepan.

5. Bring to the boil and *simmer* for 45 minutes, stirring occasionally.

6. Decant to the preserving jar and cool.

Store in a cool dark place. Once opened store in the fridge.

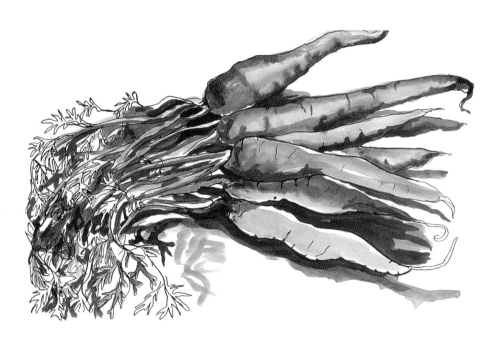

Onion Marmalade

Excellent mild pickle to accompany cold meat and Duck Terrine (q.v.).

Became very trendy in restaurants during the 80's; this recipe produces a first class version.

INGREDIENTS:

2 lbs(900g), Onions peeled and roughly chopped

2 oz(60g) Butter

1 teaspoon Salt and freshly ground Black Pepper

5 oz(140g) Caster Sugar

7 fl.oz(190ml) White Wine Vinegar

7 fl.oz(190ml) Heavy Red Wine

2 tablespoons Cassis or Ribena.

EQUIPMENT:

Big heavy stainless steel saucepan, with a close-fitting lid. A few sterilized screw-top jam jars (see Lime Pickle for method) .

METHOD:

1. Melt the butter in the saucepan, until it becomes nut-brown, but not burnt.

2. Throw in the onions, sugar and salt and pepper. Mix well.

3. Lower the heat, cover the pan and soften the onions for 40 minutes, stirring occasionally.

4. Add the wine, vinegar and Cassis. Cook slowly, uncovered, until the mixture becomes syrupy and the onions have absorbed most of the liquid. This will take about 2 hours.

5. Cool overnight.

6. Carefully remove as much surplus butter as possible from the surface.

7. Stir well and store in sterilized screw-top jam jars in a cool dark place.

Refrigerate once opened.

Makes popular cheap presents, when the jars are dressed up a bit.

Sweet and Sour Prunes

Totally delicious as an accompaniment to pates and terrines. Should be made at least a week in advance, but will continue to improve for many more. It is very important to use the best, and biggest, natural prunes you can find - not chemically treated ready to eat prunes: Sainsbury are an excellent national source.

The inclusion of tea, in some form, has developed as a substitute for dried lime blossom - which was traditional, but is not always immediately to hand!

INGREDIENTS:

1 lb(500g) big Prunes, unpitted

2 Tea Bags (Indian style)

10 oz(300g) Caster Sugar

16 fl.oz(450ml) of Tarragon flavoured White Wine Vinegar

1 whole Cinnamon Stick

2 whole Cloves

Enough Vodka to finish; this depends on the shape of your storage container (but about 5 fl.oz (150ml)

METHOD:

1. Cover the prunes with water, add the tea bags, bring to the boil, then *simmer* for 15 minutes. Allow to stand for 3 hours, by which time the fruit should have recovered it's plum-like shape. Remove the tea bags.

2. Drain the prunes. The left over liquid can be thrown away, but actually is a delicious drink and a good liquid for braising pork or *deglazing* pork chops.

3. In a stainless steel saucepan, dissolve the sugar in the vinegar, over a low heat. Add the spices and remove from the heat.

4. Gently prick eack prune a few times with a small skewer and place in a glass or stainless steel bowl (not aluminium).

5. Pour the vinegar solution over the prunes and allow to stand, at room temperature overnight.

6. Strain the vinegar into a clean stainless steel pan; bring to the boil and *simmer* for 10 minutes. Cool.

7. Sterilize a glass preserving jar - by placing it in a very low oven for 30 minutes. Remove carefully and allow to cool.

8. Place the prunes in the jar and cover with the cold vinegar; add enough vodka to completely cover the fruit, but a minimum of 5 fl.oz.

9. Seal and keep in a dark place.

Refrigerate after opening.

Pickled Plums

When plums are cheap, they can be preserved in the same manner as Sweet and Sour Prunes (q.v.). The flavouring ingredients should be changed to those listed below.

INGREDIENTS:

2 lbs(1 kilo) unbruised Plums

1 pint (600ml) White Wine Vinegar

1 lb(500g) Soft Brown Sugar

1 tablespoon(15ml) Salt

4 whole Cloves

1 whole Cinnamon Stick

1 tablespoon(15ml) Allspice Berries

1 tablespoon(15ml) Ground Ginger.

Glossary

Bain-Marie:
A bath of very hot, rather than boiling water, on to which another pan rests. This can be used for keeping food warm, or for gently cooking the contents of the top container by indirect heat: e.g. Hollandaise Sauce.

Blanch:
To cook partially, generally in boiling water (but sometimes, as for potato chips, in medium hot oil - to partially cook without browning) often for only a few seconds or minutes.

Blind, to bake:
To bake a pastry shell without its filling. To do this line the pastry case with greaseproof paper or foil, then weigh down with dry rice or beans (which can be specially kept for the purpose).

Croutes:
Slices of bread, cut into squares, triangles, rounds or hearts and toasted or fried in butter.

Croutons:
The same as above, but much smaller; often for scattering over soup.

Deglaze:
A technique used for fried or roast food, where a liquid is added to the pan and the residue at the bottom scraped away so that it blends with the liquid. This often forms the basis, or an addition to a sauce.

Diced:
To cut into small cubes.

Duxelle:
A mushroom mixture formed by the *sweating* of finely chopped mushrooms with onions or shallots, sometimes with the addition of small pieces of bacon. The whole should be cooked slowly in butter until the excess liquid evaporates.

Julienne:
Food, often vegetables, cut into matchstick-sized strips.

Marinate: (in a marinade)
To steep in a liquid (often alcohol), sometimes without completely immersing. The solids should be turned over several times.

Mirepoix:
A small dice of aromatic vegetables, used to give flavour to a cooking liquid.

Reduce:
To boil up a liquid, to diminish the volume and so increase the flavour. Be careful how much salt you add before using this procedure.

Refresh:
To put under, or in, very cold water; often to stiffen and set the colour of green vegetables, or to remove excess starch from pasta or rice.

Simmer:
To cook gently over a low flame, at just below boiling point.

Sweat:
To cook over a low heat with butter or oil, but no other liquid, until softened but not brown. Usually done with vegetables.

Index of Main Ingredients